HOW TO PREPARE A MARKETING PLAN

JOHN STAPLETON

How to Prepare a
Marketing Plan

Gower Press

First published in Britain by Gower Press Limited
140 Great Portland Street, London W1N 5TA
1971

ISBN 0 7161 0067 3

Set in 11 on 13 point Plantin and printed in Britain by
Clarke, Doble and Brendon Ltd.,
Plymouth

Contents

Illustrations

Acknowledgements

This book owes much to the many people in numerous organisations who have contributed to the thinking and the development into practice of ideas upon which it is based. It would be impossible to list all of these people by name, many of whom are probably unaware of the contribution they have made. However, mention must be made of Gilbert Cunningham of Mactac International and Donald Ingleton of Special Interest Publications, who over the years have stimulated so much thought by discussion.

My gratitude goes particularly to David Nathan, of Max Redlich Limited, who has spent many hours studying the script and making helpful suggestions. Robin Ollington, of Autonomics Limited, has transformed rudimentary form design into the practical illustrations that have been used.

I am very grateful to Keren Fraser and Heather Bond for the time they have devoted in typing and retyping the manuscript. I must also thank my friends at Autonomics Limited, who have been a constant source of encouragement and have offered much valuable advice in the construction and development of the final work.

John Stapleton

Introduction

Marketing activities are the means by which a business becomes more prosperous and, as such, are an essential cost to be borne before maximum profitability can be achieved. It is not enough to produce goods or services and make them available to the public; it is essential that markets are predetermined and a basic need converted into a positive demand. The time span between the creating of demand and its satisfaction has been considerably reduced principally because of mass production techniques and in many cases provided in advance. It is no longer practical to divert from a chosen course of action without adequate preparation and planning.

Although many businessmen have now accepted the need for greater use of marketing principles, relatively few of these businessmen fully understand where marketing fits into the traditional business organisation. Certainly the activities of marketing such as advertising, field selling and market research are not separate activities in their own right but an essential and integral part of the total business activity. Each activity is a necessary part of the total distributive function and when properly co-ordinated contributes to the general increase in the country's standard of living.

Most executives can quote the business activities which normally fall within the scope of the marketing department; those activities that come under the authority and responsibility of the marketing manager. Unfortunately too many businessmen, and even some marketing men, regard the marketing process as just a combination of such activities and that skilful manipulation will ensure business prosperity. Marketing is, however, more than an activity or group of activities; it is a state of mind which can as easily develop in the attitude of a non-marketing executive as it can with a marketing employee.

Customer-orientated executives, whether they be boffins in the laboratory or maintenance engineers on the shop floor, are essential to the successful practice of marketing within any business organisation. If increased profitability is to be achieved, one of the major objectives for the company concerned is growth. Growth is not possible without a conscious devotion to the satisfaction of market needs.

Introducing the marketing concept into any organisation will sometimes be fraught with extreme difficulty. Often a management team will appoint a marketing manager either by promoting an executive from within or by recruiting a likely candidate, with what appears to be satisfactory marketing experience, from another organisation. Once the man has been appointed the company is usually prepared, initially, to allow him considerable scope in introducing ideas and incurring additional expenditure for those activities which are universally recognised as falling within the area of marketing practice. Unless the company is extremely fortunate, this action is almost totally useless. It is tantamount to transplanting a new leg onto a person dying as a result of snake bite inflicted upon the old leg.

To become truly marketing-orientated the managing director and his management team must first evolve a definite policy of total customer awareness and a devotion to its satisfaction. Eventual introduction of the marketing man to a company inevitably means that the customer is being represented when company policy is formed. Few management teams have been able to embark upon such a course as the route has never been truly charted and the only guidance has been contained within textbooks which enumerate at length the theories and principles of marketing. As every practising executive knows they are difficult to translate into action. The first positive step is to produce the information essential for marketing decision making.

Most companies have within their own administration and control systems the basic foundations for building a management information procedure. This can be supplemented and possibly complemented by investigating the abundant amount of published information. Most industrially advanced nations have what appears to be almost unlimited sources of usable information. Apart from government publications and reports, literally thousands of useful feature articles, reports and statistical tables are published each year for businessmen by businessmen.

Rarely is this mine of information adequately used. In many companies the policy-makers are too frequently involved with the day-to-day activities of the company's operation. If any senior executive is preoccupied today with routine administrative tasks, it is likely that in the past insufficient time has been devoted to planning for today. Planning is still regarded by many as equivalent to crystal ball gazing or idle day-dreaming.

The first step in introducing effective control is the development of the marketing plan. Each of the elements of the plan can be related by the common denominator: money. It may then be measured by quantitative cost standards. Usually the marketing executive does not have the information available to do the equivalent job that would be expected of his production colleague. Every effort must be made to overcome this anomaly, particularly as in many companies over half the product selling price is spent, figuratively speaking, after the product leaves its place of manufacture.

Because of the infinite number of variables which confront the typical businessman, planning activity may never be an exact science. It is not necessary, nor perhaps desirable, for future planning to be completely scientific. Major benefits of the planning process and the measurement of opportunities come from the establishment of active procedures and the criteria against which these can be subsequently measured. By disassociating his mind from the restrictions which bind today's business operation, the executive responsible for planning should be able to see the future opportunities open to the company in greater perspective.

Generally, market research efforts have been used where management has recognised that existing communication links are unsatisfactory. There has been increasing acceptance that information is a basic raw material of marketing activities and that traditional contacts with customers are inadequate in providing the right information for decision making. Any management decision cannot possibly be implemented in complete isolation from the business. Whether it is a major capital investment in a new plant or machinery or, more simply, the appointment of an additional salesman, the consequences will have several direct and many more indirect influences upon the total business situation.

Unless a decision is made with full and detailed consideration of the known likely and possible effects of it, the management team will have lost effective control of a valuable asset and the benefits which would normally accrue to the investment made. Few businessmen would not recognise that an investment is made with a sacrifice of some alternative investment. Not only must the management team want to maximise upon the expansion it has adopted but it will need to have evidence that the action taken will prove to be the right choice. It is essential that the activities of marketing are subjected to the same thorough investigation and control as other functional activities.

Each aspect of marketing practice is an investment in time, energy and money, and must show an equitable return which can be subjected to measurement in the same way as all other business investments. By planning ahead the businessman should be able to foresee the interactive nature and consequences of critical business decisions and so ensure that all long-term plans and the decisions that resolve from these plans are properly and fully co-ordinated. Marketing helps to reduce business risks by ensuring management awareness of market needs and exploitable demand during each step of the business operation.

For a market-orientated activity to produce lasting prosperity it has to be planned systematically. Company results are dependent upon the establishment of standards and on constant research and planning with the development of objectives and suitable controls in making projections into the future. Future trends can often be predicted by the company that investigates influential factors into business performance. Rarely are the future opportunities open to a company shown as clear-cut, easily definable paths. The planner is usually confronted with an infinite number of alternatives, each of which must be fully investigated and the potential assessed.

By carefully working his way through the alternatives open to the company for those areas which, if properly exploited, become worth-while potential, the executive will have eliminated many of the prospective choices which have shown themselves to be unworthy of further consideration. In carrying out a detailed study of long-term prospects and of the forces which are likely to affect the company and its industry, the businessman has gained a far more intimate knowledge of the company and its industry and, more important, its markets, than would otherwise have been possible.

One of the arguments frequently used against marketing principles is that if attempts are made to satisfy the peculiar requirements of every customer the manufacturer will, invariably, become a provider of specials and will lose the advantages of batch or mass production. This is not necessarily contradictory to marketing principles, as the marketing concept demands that the manufacturer finds sufficient customers or potential customers with an identical special need and then provides the product for these customers. Where such a demand does not exist at a level which is attractive to the manufacturer, the product which would satisfy these prospects will not be supplied. If, however, the demand is significant, although small, and the price which the market is prepared to pay is high, the manufacturer may decide, as a conscious business decision, to produce a satisfactory product which will itself show a considerable profit margin.

OBJECTIVES OF THIS BOOK

One of the reasons for lack of formalised marketing planning in the past has been the extreme difficulty and considerable hard work necessary in putting marketing plans into a written form. The purpose of this book is to act as a trigger to encourage businessmen to develop their own marketing planning and to set up the means by which planning documentation can be developed. It is the intention to provide for businessmen, irrespective of their business function, a format against which they will be able to develop their own customer-orientated marketing operation which is based upon a definite course of action. By using the planning procedures illustrated and explained throughout this book a positive awareness of customers' needs can be developed and readers will be able to analyse, interpret and develop a programme of future planning requirements in anticipation of customer needs.

It is unlikely that any one company will need or want to use the full range of charts, diagrams and information in the pages that follow. As the needs of customers differ, so do the needs of different business organisations; whereas some companies will need to place greater emphasis on obtaining information, say, about the distribution and size of customers within their individual markets, other companies may, for example, attach greater importance to detailed sales analysis or perhaps market shares. Though few companies will use all of the information which will be possible with every single illustration, most companies should have readily available reliable information on each of the facets of planning which have been covered in individual chapters. Each chapter has been treated as an independent area for consideration and contains an introduction in the subject matter as well as explanation for each of the diagrams used.

It is hoped that this book will fill a noticeable gap in the field of management textbooks and provide a means whereby the manager can develop a programme of action to put marketing theories into practice within his own organisation. It should be useful to new managers or to students who aspire to be managers, but particularly relevant to accountants and managements anxious to measure the effectiveness of marketing action.

Development of Objectives

Few company executives have ever truly determined the business activity of their company. In defining business activity the market must be specified: who is served, why, where and when they are served, with what they are served, and how they are served. In taking this elementary step the businessman should be able to clarify in his own mind not only the limits within which opportunity should be confined but also the scope for developing the business within the fields for which experience and expertise have been developed. Determining the business activity is the first step in developing the marketing plan and is the base upon which company objectives can be developed. In order to develop a clear company policy certain aims or goals must be set. It is necessary to establish the direction in which the business must be directed and each step filled before firm company objectives are formulated.

The company objectives must not only be realistic and achievable but with short-, medium- and long-term goals shown separately. They should also be sufficiently challenging to stretch the capacity and capabilities of the executives responsible for their achievement. To be included in the marketing plan all objectives must be definable and therefore quantifiable and comparable for planning purposes.

Money is the common language of business and, is, therefore, the most suitable medium for expressing company objectives. The prime objective of any business must be the profit required. Although many companies are well known for pursuing other objectives either of a political or social nature, such objectives will be pursued only while they continue to cause an increase in profitability.

They are, therefore, secondary objectives and no more than a means to an end, although the means may well be considered laudable in their own right.

In planning a future profit requirement it will be essential to predict the sales volume required to achieve that profit. Sales are the direct result of orders and orders themselves are a result of quotations or tenders. Inquiries have to be obtained before the company can implement the chain of events which lead to the transaction being recorded in the sales ledger. By investigating historical performance, the marketing executive should be able to establish conversion ratios for each step in the chain. Once the actual amount of planned profit is agreed, the conversion ratios can be applied to indicate the sales volume needed to achieve that profit and the inquiries, quotations and orders which must be obtained before the sales can be achieved.

In determining such objectives, forecasts of likely events must be made. Every possible factor which could, conceivably, affect the business in a significant way should be considered, whether favourable or otherwise, and over which, in the short term, there can be little or no control. In listing these basic assumptions many operating problems soon become apparent to management.

All companies have their problems, for problems are the reason for the existence of decision-making managers. The difficulty facing the modern manager is not so much solving the problem as discovering its nature and cause. Often managers confuse cause with effect. Lack of sales does not necessarily mean poor selling. It could be the result of poor management planning. In overcoming business problems the company has to develop marketing strategy.

There is still much confusion among businessmen, between marketing strategy and marketing tactics. Strategy is the art of preparing the company's resources to ensure maximum sales penetration upon which company profitability is so dependent. It means understanding the buying habits, attitudes and characteristics of potential customers. It is capitalising on the strength and weakness of competitors. Tactics, however, are the methods employed in face-to-face dealings with customers and prospective customers.

One contributory cause of confusion between strategy and tactics is the interdependence of certain activities. In pricing, for example, the company may decide to slot into a particular price level – the level it decides is the most vulnerable for exploitation. This is strategy. Once the price level has been established, necessary variations in the unit price from day to day are tactical.

Figure 1.1 Financial objectives
This is in essence a rudimentary planned profit statement. It is the basis upon which the company's future plans are to be established and should be used as a trigger document for the development of company policy in future years. It is a dynamic document which compels discipline on the total marketing operation both in philosophy and in operation.

The insertion of objectives for year one beside objectives for year five is a deliberate attempt to divorce long-term objectives from those which are developed for the immediate future. In looking ahead it is too easy to build upon historical information and simply extend an established trend forward. In the development of objectives it is advisable for management to consider the future without being hindered by current ideas, philosophies, operations and systems. At this early stage in the development of the company's marketing plan it is suggested that executives should establish

FINANCIAL OBJECTIVES

Date   Prepared by

Prior Year Actual			Current Year Budget			Activity	Current Year Forecast			Objectives Year One			Objectives Year Five		
£ value	% total	% growth	£ value	% total	% growth		£ value	% total	% growth	£ value	% total	% growth	£ value	% total	% growth
						Sales product group A									
						Group B									
						Group C									
						Group D									
						Total sales									
						Gross margin									
						Marketing expense									
						1 Salaries and wages									
						2 Vehicles									
						3 Publicity									
						4 Rent and rates									
						5 Commissions									
						6 Depreciation									
						7 Government charges									
						8 Taxes									
						9 Interest charges									
						10 Other expense									
						Net profit									
						Employees:									
						Management and supervision									
						Salesmen									
						Administration									
						Clerical									
						Other									
						Order input									
						Total assets									
						Return on assets									

FINANCIAL OBJECTIVES SUPPORTING DATA

Date

Prepared by

Prior Year Actual			Current Year Budget			Activity	Current Year Forecast			Objectives Year One			Objectives Year Five		
£ value	% GM	% growth	£ value	% GM	% growth		£ value	% GM	% growth	£ value	% GM	% growth	£ value	% GM	% growth
						Sales group 'A' home									
						Export									
						New									
						Established									
						Sales group 'B' home									
						Export									
						New									
						Established									
						Sales group 'C' home									
						Export									
						New									
						Established									
						Sales group 'D' home									
						Export									
						New									
						Established									
						Marketing expense									
						Home									
						Export									
						New									
						Established									
						Sales price index home									
						Export									
						Market share home									
						Export									

for themselves, without preconceived doctrines, the position that they would like to see the company adopt five years hence, then start to consider the ways in which the financial objectives can be achieved.

The illustration necessarily is expressed in purely monetary terms but will normally be the result of much deliberation and discussion between senior executives. A full report will be prepared before the actual objectives, in terms of action, are put into financial terms. Actual objectives will vary from company to company, but certain aims or goals are shown here as a guide.

Figure 1.2   Financial objectives supporting data

This is another policy statement showing basic operational details, each of which constitutes a fundamental formulation of forward policy. It is used to provide more detailed information of the financial objectives, but is prepared separately from the previous illustration, so that when detailed forecasts are produced they can be related to these final statements of intent. Where the sales forecasts differ substantially from the preliminary objectives contained within this document, management must consider deeply methods by which the company's performance can be improved by either increased productivity or, perhaps, the launch of a new product.

The sales price index is introduced as a control to avoid distortion in sales performance by inflation. By declaring the desired market share the company becomes aware of its expected performance compared with the performance of the industry as a whole.

Figure 1.3   Order input plan

This is not only a vital control document, it is also a necessary work sheet in the development of production control and programming. In this particular diagram planned orders and the expected gross margin are shown by quarters, because, during the development phase of the marketing plan, quarterly assessment should help to eliminate distortion through variation in monthly order input. It is also easier to relate trends over a longer period of time and to establish more definite patterns of growth.

Many customers place regular orders for delivery at set periods and, in some industries, delivery periods may be extended over a year or more. For these companies a large part of their future sales are already on the books as orders for future delivery. Such orders appear in the section "orders received" and should be included according to their forecast delivery date. The additional orders required are those orders in terms of value which are needed to meet the company targets.

The combined figures of orders received and orders required should always exceed the amount of sales forecasted. Companies grow day by day, and on average the daily order value should always slightly exceed that of the previous day. This means that the orders on hand at the end of each period should always be greater than the orders on hand at the previous period and that there will always be a gradual broadening between the financial value of sales and the financial value of orders. In the same way a company with a standard three months' delivery period will always have at least three months' value of orders in the pipeline.

Gross margins are shown in this document, so that priorities in terms of choice in planning production can be established and directed towards those products which provide the greatest gross margin contribution.

Figure 1.4   Assumptions, problems, opportunities, strategies
This is a simple form which is justified by the necessity to discipline management's thinking towards positive and measurable attempts at considering the many alternative opportunities available.

The form is capable of many variations but it is essential that the financial costs of assumptions, problems and opportunities are clearly recorded year by year, and cumulatively, so that financial returns on investment can be clearly assessed. The costs of alternative strategies will be clearly indicated if the results to gross margins are stated. It is necessary to show these over the full five-year cycle as, in practice, different strategies bring in different returns at different times during the life cycle of a product. Sometimes a heavy initial investment in strategy will bring a higher return in the medium to long term. Under some circumstances the company will have to decide whether it wants to finance the initial costs from its present cash flow and use the restricted amount of money available from funds, or to borrow additional working capital in anticipation of repaying debts out of future revenue in the expectation of higher returns.

Figure 1.5   Analysis of profit improvements
Every business must plan to improve its profitability by increased productivity and it should make a positive effort to improve its performance in expenditure, of fixed and variable costs, and by revenue

FIGURE 1.3

ORDER INPUT PLAN

DATE:　　　　　　　　　　　　　　　　　　　　　　　PREPARED BY:

CATEGORY	YEAR ONE £000's										YEAR TWO £000's									
	Orders Value					Gross Margin					Orders Value					Gross Margin				
	Quarters				Full	Quarters				Full	Quarters				Full	Quarters				Full
	1st	2nd	3rd	4th	Year	1st	2nd	3rd	4th	Year	1st	2nd	3rd	4th	Year	1st	2nd	3rd	4th	Year
Orders on Hand – Total																				
Product Group 'A'																				
Orders Received																				
Orders Required																				
Class of Customer I																				
II																				
III																				
Product Group 'B'																				
Orders Received																				
Orders Required																				
Class of Customer I																				
II																				
III																				
Product Group 'C'																				
Orders Received																				
Orders Required																				
Class of Customer I																				
II																				
III																				
Product Group 'D'																				
Orders Received																				
Orders Required																				
Class of Customer I																				
II																				
III																				
Total Orders Received																				
Total Orders Required																				
Less Sales for Period																				
O.O.H. End of Period																				

FIGURE 1.4 DATE:	ASSUMPTIONS, PROBLEMS, OPPORTUNITIES STRATEGIES PREPARED BY:									
	PROJECTION 1 – 5 YEARS									
	Year One	CUM	Year Two	CUM	Year Three	CUM	Year Four	CUM	Year Five	CUM
ASSUMPTION										
PROBLEM										
OPPORTUNITY										
STRATEGIES 1.										
GROSS MARGIN 2.										
GROSS MARGIN 3.										
GROSS MARGIN										

by higher prices and sales expansion. It is only by recording and implementing profit improvement efforts that a company is able to investigate and analyse the present operation in the search for profit improvement and potential.

Figure 1.6 Planned changes, profit performance
Many events will affect future profit performance and those shown in this illustration are typical of many businesses. By recognising the likely effect of these changes upon the business the company is able to actively pursue remedial action.

   Although the factors which affect changes in profit performance are numerous, for most businesses the more usual influences and certainly the most significant can be isolated. The major headings shown in this illustration are the usual elements affecting profitability; forecasts of their likely effects when made will prepare management for changes in the ratios encountered among operating costs.

FIGURE 1.5

ANALYSIS OF PROFIT IMPROVEMENTS

DATE: PREPARED BY:

Income and Expense Analysis	Prior Yr. Actual	Current Year Budget	Current Year Forecast	Prior Year Actual = 100 Selling Price Changes	Purchase Price Changes	Wage Rate Changes	Productivity Agreements	Sales Expansion Products	Sales Expansion by S.I.C.	Stock Valuation	Depreciation	Currency Exchange	Total Changes
Year One													
Purchases													
Works Costs													
Sales Group 'A'													
'B'													
'C'													
'D'													
Gross Margin													
Marketing Expense													
Stock													
W.I.P.													
Value													
/////	/////	/////	/////	/////	/////	/////	/////	/////	/////	/////	/////	/////	/////
Year Five													
Purchases													
Works Costs													
Sales Group 'A'													
'B'													
'C'													
'D'													
Gross Margin													
Marketing Expense													
Stock													
W.I.P.													
Value													

FIGURE 1.6

PLANNED CHANGES PROFIT PERFORMANCE

DATE: PREPARED BY:

ACTIVITY	Change Prior Year	
	Year One	Year Five
	£	£
Selling Price Increases		
Selling Price Decreases		
Purchase Price Changes		
Wage Rate Changes		
Productivity Agreements		
Stock Valuation		
Depreciation		
Currency Exchange		
Other		
Change in Profit Performance		

2 Preparation of the Sales Forecast

The sales forecast is the basis of the total marketing plan. Preparing a sales forecast is not just a matter of looking at historical sales and attempting to establish trends, but an effort to look into the future and to estimate market sales potential. In assessing the future and endeavouring to predict what products the market will demand and what new modern products, or product innovations, will be required to satisfy that demand, a company has begun to be objective about its future. Obviously many of the techniques used are purely subjective in nature, but by establishing targets which are realistic and obtainable, and which will show an acceptable profit return, the company will be eliminating many of the numerous variables which face every business, and, if properly organised, will tend to reduce the risk element.

A forecast based on market sales potential is based on future customer requirements and is a measurement of the needs of the market for a definite period into the future. Every effort is made to predict changes in pattern of demand and on recent events of the immediate past which have not yet been sufficiently significant in total or over an adequate period of time for a trend to become clearly established. It will make full allowance for new applications in established markets and for innovations in new markets. In looking into the future it is necessary to disassociate the mind from traditional product concepts and to think more specifically about the product or service which the company can provide and which is consistent with the determined business activity.

The period which companies choose for their sales forecast may vary from five years to twenty years. For most companies five years is the most appropriate time span and, as many products which will be sold in five years' time are already established within the present product range, it is normally possible to use historical sales performance on which projections into the future can be based. Such a projection is dependent upon future events being similar to events which have happened in the past. Due allowance must be made for changes in general economic conditions and for changes in competitive forces within the industry which serves the company's market.

The projections need to be subjected to detailed evaluation of why the trends have appeared and how relevant they will be in the future. Published economic data can be used to compare movements, either short-term fluctuations or medium- to long-term trends within the total market. Sometimes acceptable degrees of correlation can be traced. These tied indicators become useful parameters in forecasting. If a company is able to correlate industry sales to a published statistic and that statistic is subjected to medium- to long-term forecasting techniques from a reliable source, any forecast based upon such figures can become most significant to the company's planning.

The sales forecast may be as sophisticated or as simple as is justified by the business. The techniques borrowed from other disciplines such as operational research are complex in themselves, but may be used to simplify forecasting. These techniques are more often used by larger organisations with diverse products and markets. The small- to medium-sized business is better able to maintain close contact with its markets and, as such, is able to monitor immediately any likely changes in demand. For this reason the smaller business may use elementary forecasting methods which can often produce better results than those employed by the larger company where contact with customers has become separated by longer lines of communication.

Because of the expense involved, and the considerable skill required in preparing sales forecasts, the larger company will carry out its own research using its own specially recruited personnel. The smaller business cannot justify economically such recruitment and will usually commission elementary research from specialist agencies.

In recent years multi-client projects have become particularly significant and there is every indication that their growing acceptance will continue. In spreading the cost of research over a number of sponsors it is possible for the research company to employ highly skilled people and to carry out projects in considerable depth across a broad front. In addition, many of these agencies will prepare a report that will be confidential to the sponsor concerned. Such a report will indicate to management, in a detailed and unbiased manner, the image that their company has developed. It will show how they are regarded as manufacturers, in the eyes of present customers and potential customers, as a future investment and even, perhaps, as an employer. The sponsor firm will be able to discover why a company is winning business and under what circumstances business is lost. Management is given the opportunity to assess product acceptability and the effectiveness of its marketing activities when compared to major competitors.

These multi-client projects are proving of increasing value to users and their increasing acceptance in industry is a sure sign of the recognition by businessmen of the need for research into such areas as market size, market growth rates, the factors affecting market change, market shares broken down by application and type of product, and the decision-making process leading to purchase. Usually these research projects will identify the normal sources of supply, market shares held by individual suppliers, the various product specifications, and, frequently, the most suitable means of communication by publicity and the sales force.

While more and more businessmen are becoming convinced of the need to produce forecasts, few feel competent to tackle forecasts of the volume likely to be achieved in overseas territories. Marketing practitioners no longer use the expression "export markets" because the word "market" means one segment of a total market open to penetration, irrespective of geographical boundaries. In principle, there is no difference between home and overseas areas, and it is only the application of research techniques and the implementation of those techniques which distinguish one geographical area from another. In preparing the market sales potential for an overseas territory the executive must make allowances for an increased number of variables likely to be encountered. He should draw a distinction in each territory between expatriate salesmen and performance achieved by natives, that achieved by competitors at home and that achieved by others.

He must also investigate and include details of the vested interests which the country concerned has to protect, and any possible political interference. Frequently the durability of forecasts will vary from country to country, for forecasts by para-governmental bodies in industrially advanced nations have more stability than those by countries undergoing rapid economic and social change. Certainly he should make allowances for the degree of sophistication of the national statistics produced by each country.

Whatever the market segment or geographical area to be investigated and for which forecasts are to be prepared, the major benefits accruing to the businessman follow the detailed consideration of sales opportunities which should produce clear indications of the company's future prospects.

The object of sales forecasting must be clearly defined at the outset. These are quite distinct from the company objectives, covered in Chapter 1, and are intended, primarily, to establish quite clearly and unequivocably the whole purpose and detail of the company sales forecast. The objectives must take the form of a clear brief on the extent and detail of the forecast and the amount of time and money which can be justified in development. By defining objectives it is possible to avoid the natural tendency to break down the forecast within predetermined limits based upon traditional or conventional parameters.

Sales forecasts must be prepared in such a form as to show how the company's marketing strategy can be used to increase sales and volume and at what cost in terms of time, money and effort, and the profitability which will accrue at various levels of sales performance.

Any sales forecast is subject to numerous influential factors which must be isolated and capable of measurement according to some predetermined standard. While the variables facing the businessman can be related almost to infinity, certain influential factors have considerably more effect than

Figure 2a											
NEW PRODUCT INVESTMENT											

Market Segment	Number of Establishments	Sales Value	Sales potential Current Year	Sales potential Plan Year Five	Gross Margin	Total Investment Required					% Return on Investment Five Years
						R & D	Plant	Selling	Publicity	Total	
Manufacturing											
Distribution											
Finance and Credit											
Service											
Total											

FIGURE 2.1

SALES AND GROSS MARGIN ANALYSIS BY PRODUCT AND MARKET SEGMENT

DATE: A = Sales and Value   B = Gross Margin %   C = Growth Prior Year 2 = 100   PREPARED BY:

Prior Yr. 2 Actual			Prior Yr. 1 Actual			Current Yr. Forecast			Activity	Plan Year One			Plan Year Two			Plan Year Three			Plan Year Four			Plan Year Five		
A	B	C	A	B	C	A	B	C	Product Group	A	B	C	A	B	C	A	B	C	A	B	C	A	B	C
									Total Sales															
									Market Segment															
									Total Sales															

others. The forecaster must endeavour to isolate the factors and grade them according to their significance in such a way that weightings can be applied and an acceptable forecast be determined within tolerable limits.

Many businessmen confuse a forecast of market sales potential with their own company forecast or targets. They should appreciate that every company recognises the fundamental need for growth, and is struggling to increase its markets. This happens even in a declining or static market and, inevitably, leads to some company failure. In forecasting there is nearly always a bias towards one's own company and this tendency must be avoided, otherwise operating budgets, which are based on sales forecasts, will be overestimated and profitability will suffer.

In the struggle to increase market shares some of the competing companies may resort to pricing tactics in order to overcome their marketing deficiency, and this will, inevitably, lead to an industrial profit decline. Companies which remain strong during this situation are those which have planned their strategy on tangible customer benefits which can be provided economically and for which the customer is willing to pay a premium. The forecaster will normally avoid bias towards his own company and products if he applies the same standard of measurement for any element of strategy to be used against competitive companies and their products.

In preparing a forecast it is necessary to predict market sales potential based not only on general economic conditions, but also on the interplay of total competitive activity, which often causes an expansion of the total market, before deciding the individual strengths and weaknesses of the major competitors in the market place.

Forecasts must also be made of trends in related industries which provide indirect competition to the company's own products and which may be an influential factor in the growth rate of the industry concerned. To do this the businessman must concentrate initially upon total demand and the various applications which will satisfy that demand. He should then simplify that demand into those products which are directly competitive to his own, not only at the present but also during the period of the forecast. It is at this stage that the forecaster should be able to discover opportunities for product innovation or for new product development.

Figure 2a   New product investment.   New products are the future life blood of the company and their discovery, development and production are necessary parts of the sales forecasting programme. This process is simplified if the company has determined its business activity, developed its objectives and prepared its sales forecasts based on a systematic planning process.

Figure 2.1   Sales and gross margin analysis by product and market segment

In developing a forecast it is necessary to provide a base year on which an industry can be projected. In using a full year of actual sales performance achieved two years ago, and by using prices which were current at that time, it is possible to develop forecasts which are related year by year and which are exactly comparable over the full period of the forecast. At this stage of the forecast it is not necessary to think in terms of sales volume as opposed to value, for price increases are discounted, leaving growth margin percentages consistent for each year of the forecast period.

It is necessary to include gross margin percentages as a control measure against anticipated sales. In this illustration sales performance is divided into product groups as a first step towards production programming. In addition, forecasts are shown in market segments which will be in groups or categories appropriate to the company concerned but ideally should be some combination of groupings within the standard industrial classification. Predicted sales for five years hence can be tabulated in outline for each product group to be recorded.

Figure 2.2   Sales and gross margin year forecast

This forecast shows historical sales for each of two full years in the past and apportions sales performance for the next full year by 4 three-monthly periods. Once again the sales value is shown with the appropriate gross margins. Market segments are also clearly indicated, as these are a necessary source of information for sales planning and promotional activities. This one-year forecast should be shown in considerable detail, not only for production planning purposes but also to enable the financial controller to arrange a realistic cash flow.

Figure 2.3   Sales barometer

Frequently companies with an adverse actual sales performance against forecast find that remedial action, no matter how successful, is too late to bring the company back on a profitable course and worth-while sales opportunities are lost. This chart is a control document which can indicate performance only after sales have appeared on the sales ledger.

In order to avoid such consequences the businessman must develop early warning signals. As inquiries, quotations and orders have been set as part of company objectives it is necessary only

FIGURE 2.2

SALES AND GROSS MARGIN YEAR FORECAST

DATE: PREPARED BY:

Prior Yr 2 Actual		Prior Yr 1 Actual		Current Yr. Forecast		Activity	Qtr 1		Qtr 2		Qtr 3		Qtr 4		Full Plan Year One	
value	GM	value	GM	value	GM	Product	value	GM	value	GM	value	GM	value	GM	value	GM
						Market Segment										

Figure 2.3								SALES BAROMETER									
DATE:											Month			PREPARED BY:			
Prior Year Same Period	Prior Year Same Period Cumulative	Product		Budget Month	Budget Month Cumulative	Current Month Actual	Current Month Actual Cumulative	Variance Current/Budget	Variance Current/Budget Cumulative	Next Month Budget	Next Month Budget Cumulative	Next Month Revised Forecast	Next Month Revised Forecast Cumulative	Variance Budget/Forecast	Variance Budget/Forecast Cumulative	Full Year Budget	Full Year Forecast

to split the objectives into equal periods for the year sales are forecast and programme them according to the established ratios, making full allowance for the time-lag between each element in the conversion of inquiry into sales, for early warning signals to be established.

The sales barometer must not only include the part performance of the company by months, but must also indicate the general trend established month by month cumulatively throughout the sales year. In this way it is possible to establish clear trends within one sales year. Many business-men fail to appreciate that growth in sales does not happen in one year but goes on, day by day, week by week and month by month. By establishing trends in this way it is possible to make revised forecasts for the following period and a cumulative revised forecast for the year-end. Obviously, if the revised year-end forecast shows a decline compared to budget, the marketing contingency plan must be brought into operation.

Figure 2.4 New product requirements/developments

To maintain a constant growth rate it is essential for each company to estimate the life cycle of each product in its range and to ensure that a new product has been launched to coincide with the apex of the established product's sales cycle so as to continue the company growth rate as the established product begins its decline.

New products should not be introduced in a haphazard fashion but at a predetermined time in the company's expansion programme.

New product introduction should be based on demand established by original research and on observed market needs, developed according to their sales potential, cost of development, and promotion. Each new product must be looked upon as a total investment in company funds; resources and executive time must be charged to the new product development programme in a reasonable and equitable basis. The figure illustrated should be considered as a special profit and loss account for new product-type demands and should be costed accordingly.

Figure 2.5 New product launch

One of the techniques which most companies could borrow from operational research scientists is a network analysis for launching a new product. So many different elements are essential for a successful launch and are dependent upon each being completed at particular times. Some companies have found it expedient to try a product in a test marketing area in order to iron out many of the difficulties.

Figure 2.6 Economic indicators

No company operates in complete isolation. Effects of the national economy and world trade in general have to be considered in the development of detailed forecasts of market sales potential and market share which the investigating company plans to achieve. This illustration lists many of the usual indicators.

FIGURE 2.4

NEW PRODUCT REQUIREMENTS/DEVELOPMENTS

DATE: PREPARED BY:

	Plan Year One		Plan Year Two		Plan Year Three		Plan Year Four		Plan Year Five	
	value	GM	value	GM	value	GM	value	GM	value	GM
Forecast Established Markets Sales Potential										
Forecast New Markets Sales Potential										
Forecast Sales Potential by Penetration										
Forecast Company Sales Expansion										
Planned Company Sales Expansion										
Variances										
Planned Product Innovations										
Changes in G.M. – Sales Required										
Net variances										
Marketing Research Expenditure										
Research and Development Expense										
Additional Sales requirement										
New Products in Section – Established										
New Products in Section – New										
Demand Forecasts										
Product Type A										
Product Type B										
Product Type C										
Product Type D										
Total										
Additional Marketing Expense										
Final Sales Forecast										
Forecast Market Share										
Changes in Net Profit										

FIGURE 2.5

NEW PRODUCT LAUNCH

DATE: PREPARED BY:

PACKAGING	Test Launch	National Launch
Packs, Labels	Research – Re–design – Costings – Final Selection	
Outers, Display	Test – Final Specification	
Point of Sale	Select Outlets – Collate Results – Analyse – Select	Selling Through
THE PRODUCT		
Specification	Actual Costings – Popular Sizes – Revise – Production Trials	
Colour, Shape	Acceptability – Revision – Test – Final Specification	
DISTRIBUTION		
Outlets	Wholesalers/Distributors/Agents – Discounts – Retail	Significant Distribution
Sales Force	Merchandising Training – Test Discounts – National Preparation	Buyers – Merchandising
Sales Services	Prepare Vehicles – Deliver Stocks – Journey Routes	Trial Discount, Trial Offers
PUBLICITY		
Consumers	Test Launch – Develop Campaign Objectives	National Press TV
Trade	Direct Mail – Public Relations – Product Potential	Trade – Technical
Others	Trade Associations – Technical Press – Vested Interest	Press Releases
MARKETING		
RESEARCH		
Quantitive	Stock Movement – Distribution Analysis – Consumer Audits	Distribution Studies
Consumer		
Acceptance	Store Questioning – Analyses of Buying Groups – Repeats	Repeat Purchase Trends
Desk Analysis	Sales Penetration – Seasonal Variation – Product Awareness	Distribution Costings
MARKETING		
DECISIONS	Sales Performance – Trade – Consumer – Budgets – Approval	Performance Against Forecast

SALES CONFERENCE

FIGURE 2.6			ECONOMIC INDICATORS						
DATE:					PREPARED BY:				
Prior Year 2	Prior Year 1	Current Year	Activity		Plan Year 1	Plan Year 2	Plan Year 3	Plan Year 4	Plan Year 5
			Company Sales						
			Industry Sales						
			Gross National Product						
			GNP Per Capita						
			Population						
			Working Population						
			Index of Hours Worked						
			Index of Wages						
			Index of Raw Materials						
			Cost of Living Index						
			Index of Wholesale Prices						
			Balance of Trade						
			Balance of Payments						
///	///	///	Investment		///	///	///	///	///
			1. Manufacturing & Construction						
			2. Other Private Industries						
			3. Nationalised Industries						
			4. Stock Building						
			5. Housing						
			6. Roads						
			7. Other Public Services						
			8. Transfer Costs Land & Building						
			Defence						
			Consumption – Personal						
			Social & Public Services						
			Exports						
			Imports						

3 Appraisal of Competitor Profiles

There is only one element in the modern business environment which has any marked degree of certainty and that is the certainty of change. It may be change in the size of a market or its structure, or among the firms operating within the market, or the markets with which it is concerned.

No company or organisation in a free society operates in complete isolation, for even monopolies struggle against competition for available purchasing power. Opposition may come from a substitute product or companies providing products or services which indirectly affect performance. With the customers' available funds as the target for suppliers ranging from paper clips to computers, establishing the cause and effect of the forces of competition becomes more and more critical as the degree of complexity of influential factors increases. In order to make an assessment of these factors it is necessary to isolate those which are likely to be most significant in their impact upon the market place.

Price cutting is the most frequently encountered of all tactical devices in the struggle against competition. This is a negative approach unless the company has made the price cut from a position of strength and anticipates growth in the total market because of increased consumption as a direct result of the price promotion, which will increase its profit.

Product innovation which brings a product closer to the needs of the market will, until it is copied by others, often cause a shift in purchasing habits towards the innovating company. Sometimes consumers will begin to use a substitute because the other product is in short supply or because the substitute has become available at a price which compares favourably against that of the original.

The Government, in producing new legislation, will frequently create a new market or cause a substantial growth or, maybe, decline in established markets in its attempt to improve the social and economic life of the nation. Sudden changes in taste or fashion usually cause sudden shifts in demand from one source of supply to another. Variations in the climate or fluctuations in the temperature can seriously affect the sales of products which rely upon extremes of temperature for sales volume. Trade recessions, strikes or industrial disputes often bring in their wake changes in purchasing habits.

Fortunately, many of these influences are predictable. Certainly there will be any amount of published comment indicating likely possibilities. Occasionally trade associations and professional institutions sponsor investigations into future events, and numerous authoritative writers produce

FIGURE 3.1	FINANCIAL PERFORMANCE						
DATE:					PREPARED BY:		
COMPANY	PRIOR YEAR ACTUAL £000's				NET PROFIT % RETURN ON		
Company & Competitors	Sales	Net Income	Total Assets	Ordinary Shares	Sales	Total Assets	Ordinary Shares
Company Performance							
/////	/////	/////	/////	/////	/////	/////	/////

FIGURE 3.2.

STANDARD COMPARISON

DATE: PREPARED BY:

Competitor	Prior Year = 100	Capital	Reserves	Long Term Loans	Funds Employed	Stock in Hand	Work in Progress	Debtors	Cash in Hand	Current Assets	Creditors	Bank Overdraft	Current Taxation	Preference Dividends	Ordinary Share Divs.	Current Liabilities	Net Current Assets	Investment Associates	Investments Subsids.	Other Investments	Current Investments	Depreciation	Goodwill	Total Fixed Assets	Mgnt. & Supervision	Office & Administration	Manufacturing Labour	Salesmen	Total Manpower	Agents & Distributors	Manufact'rg Plant Sq Ft	Advert'sg Appropriation	Sales Office	Warehouses	Distribution Vehicles
Company A																																			
Company B																																			
Company C																																			
Company D																																			
Company E																																			

thousands of words in feature articles, news columns, and special reports which can be of value to the businessman looking into the future. While it is not always possible to forecast accurately the likely consequences of any of these events, it is still possible to prepare remedial measures in advance, at different levels of effectiveness. If the consequences of such events are quantified in monetary terms, the businessman will be able to equate consequences with sales volume and hence profitability. At this point the contingency plan may be brought into operation.

Very few businessmen have yet developed a full and comprehensive reference library of published information. An index of many such sources is contained in Appendix 1.

A major, but as yet unused, source of valuable information is universities' business studies departments. Students carry out detailed investigations into industry as part of their studies and their lecturers are often prolific writers and business consultants in their own right in a part-time capacity. They are often encouraged by their university or college to develop and maintain contact with industry. The information they obtain is not usually published, but will frequently be made available to those persons who have developed good relationships with the colleges.

In investigating and charting the information on competitors, as illustrated in this chapter, a company is forced to assess its competition and its activities in purely financial terms, enabling the company to make comparisons and to develop a standard against which its own performance can be measured. In addition, the detailed investigation necessary to complete the forms creates a self-educating process and will enable managers to plan their future operations based upon the collective experience of the major suppliers and their market or markets. It will also enable the planner to quantify the interactive forces of competition.

Figure 3.1 Financial performance

This simple chart is intended to highlight the profitability and growth of significant suppliers and to compare their performance against each other. There are in existence organisations which provide considerable detail of the financial performance of companies operating within a given industry but information is made available to subscribers anonymously. Nevertheless this material is invaluable for comparative studies and for planning purposes.

Before analysing the published information on competitors it is advisable for the investigator to prepare definitions for each of the headings in this chart. Sales can mean different things to different companies. Net income for any company at any one time can be influenced by such things as stock evaluation, and total assets are often subject to considerable degrees of variation of interpretation among accountants. Accountants also disagree about the true meaning of profit and for any one company profit performance may vary substantially according to the accounting procedure preferred.

Share prices are usually dependent upon the value of distributed dividends and they will not always be a direct reflecion of a company's profitability. Share prices can fluctuate widely in any given period and it may be misleading to adopt a share valuation at any one time. It may be more realistic to take a mean average over a full year, but allow more weighting for the most recent period of trading.

Figure 3.2   Standard comparison

This document is equivalent to a direct comparison of the detailed profit and loss account of each major competitor. Certain items listed will be impossible to extract from published information and, unless the information is obtainable from a reliable unofficial source, the executive concerned must attempt to make an evaluation based upon judgement. If this technique is used he must qualify the assessment and justify it in logical terms, otherwise it is best ignored altogether until such time as the information becomes available.

By providing an index, in which the prior year to that being prepared is equal to 100, the businessman is able to compare successive years against each other and also the relative growth of each asset or investment.

Figure 3.3   Weighted services and performance

In making a comparision between competitive firms it is logical to assume that whatever the extent of market penetration achieved by those firms the success or otherwise of their achievements is attributable to some activity on their part. One company may have a strong sales force, another may spend considerable sums on advertising. Whatever the cause, it should be isolated. In drawing up a "league table" of competitors, businessmen should develop the means of weighting these activities. The factors which are typical of competing companies are shown in this illustration.

In order to develop a realistic appraisal so that one activity can be compared against a dissimilar activity, weighting techniques are used. Although each of the factors is totally interdependent

COMPANY		Price	Technical Specification	Delivery Services	Packaging	Supporting Services	Company Reputation	Product Reputation	Reciprocal Trade Agreements	Captive Markets	Personal Relationships	Outside Influences	Product Performance	Finish Design	Length of Service	Advertising & Public Relations	Merchandising	Sales Strength	Sales Ability	Channels of Distribution	Total Assessment
OWN COMPANY																					
	SALES	£																			
	SALES	£				%	TOTAL SALES				MARKET SHARE										
	SALES	£				%	TOTAL SALES				MARKET SHARE										
	SALES	£				%	TOTAL SALES				MARKET SHARE										
	SALES	£				%	TOTAL SALES				MARKET SHARE										
	SALES	£				%	TOTAL SALES				MARKET SHARE										
COMMENTS																					

FIGURE 3.3

WEIGHTED SERVICES AND PERFORMANCE

DATE:

PREPARED BY:

D

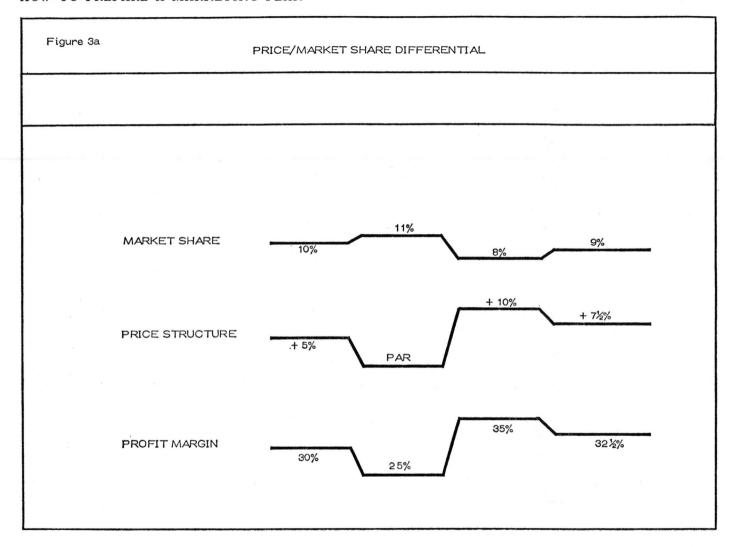

Figure 3a

PRICE/MARKET SHARE DIFFERENTIAL

MARKET SHARE

11%
10%
8%
9%

PRICE STRUCTURE

+ 10%
+ 5%
PAR
+ 7½%

PROFIT MARGIN

35%
30%
2 5%
32½%

and the mix unique to each company, it is subject to constant variation. Studying each factor the businessman will decide the significance of each activity so that the relevance of, say, price can be compared to sales ability or sales strength.

In the context of this chart the price referred to is a strategic one. The technical specification is the inherent characteristic of the product, any one of which if properly exploited can be the foundation for the establishment of a unique selling proposition.

"Delivery service" may be the means that are adopted, such as road, rail, sea or air, and may also include the speed of delivery and frequency. The emphasis on packaging is not only restricted to the strength or durability of the container but also to its aesthetic design. Supporting services will include such facilities as credit agreements, leasing facilities, consultancy or installation. Often, when faced with a purchasing decision, a buyer may choose a particular proposition simply because it has originated from a well-established company which is known to him and in which he has confidence. Similarly, products that have become well entrenched and accepted in the market place may often be chosen in preference to products that may be superior but are not so well known.

The practice of reciprocal trade agreements has not been well publicised but is established although hidden by pretence of some other arrangement. Some companies have engaged in vertical integration by taking over customers, so ensuring a certain outlet for their products. Because it is captive, sales opportunities will not be left open to competitors. Many businesses have prospered in the past because of personal relationships between prominent members of the firm. This advantage frequently disappears with the departure of one of the individuals involved. Some companies make a positive effort to cultivate other organisations which could have a non-competing but nevertheless a vested interest in identical markets. These concerns are frequently able to exercise considerable influence over buying decisions.

Many manufacturers tend to take their products for granted and rarely investigate the use to which they are being put by customers and how relevant the products are to customers' applications. Often, research establishes that features introduced in good faith by a manufacturer are not used by the customer although they have paid for them in the selling price.

They may not have recognised their significance nor relevance to them at the time of purchase. In assessing the product's performance the businessman must relate application to product characteristics. Many companies have developed their own market share as a direct result of superior finish or design for their product. Buyers can be impressed by stories of long life for certain items, particularly in the mechanical field, and will often make a purchasing decision because the cost of the equipment can be spread over many years of operation.

In some industries, advertising is the most significant factor in influencing sales performance, particularly where expenditure is supported by creative expertise and by shrewd media selection. Merchandising is a comparatively new term, although many of the techniques have been practised since the earliest days of trading. Their prominence has been achieved largely as a result of greater use of advertising, particularly by television where emphasis at the point of sale has become a necessity. The adoption of the "silent salesman" continues to improve. Sales strength relates clearly to the numbers employed, while the section on sales ability relates directly to the knowledge and the skill in its use by sales personnel. Not every company distributes its products through identical channels. Some use distributors or stockists, others may deliver direct to the retailer or even the ultimate consumer. Different channels have varying degrees of competence in selling their suppliers' products and their effectiveness can be critical to the sales volume achieved by any one company.

Figure 3a   Price/market share differential. In arriving at a final assessment, based upon established standards relating each factor to every other factor, the executive is able to compare the total significance of these in terms of market share and will be able to relate the performance of individual companies according to the factor or factors upon which they concentrate.

Figure 3.4   Geographical sales distribution
Many sales regions used by companies have grown from historical foundations. In fact, they should be closely related to a significant activity, such as the regions used by the Department of Trade and Industry enabling measurement against figures it provides, or it could use the regions adopted by television companies so that regional television campaigns carry maximum cost effectiveness.

Figure 3b   Market analysis. Breaking down a total geographical area into significant regions ensures that the company can vet performance and provide monitoring systems. Thus adverse performance in any one region can be remedied at the earliest possible time. Certainly, where performances vary from one period to the next within certain regions, the cause can be isolated and positive action taken to counteract it.

FIGURE 3.4

GEOGRAPHICAL SALES DISTRIBUTION

DATE:

PREPARED BY:

COMPANY (By Product Group)		Northern	Yorkshire & Humberside	East Anglia	South East	G.L.C.	South West	Wales	North West	Scotland	Northern Ireland	Total Home Market	Overseas Area A	Overseas Area B	Overseas Area C	Total Overseas	Total Sales
	£000s sales																
	% total																
	£000s sales																
	% total																
	£000s sales																
	% total																
	£000s sales																
	% total																
	£000s sales																
	% total																
	£000s sales																
	% total																

AREAS

CODE

1	**NORTH AND SCOTLAND**	**2,287**
11	Cumberland	97
12	County Durham	383
13	Northumberland	250
14	Westmorland	20
15	Scotland	1,537
2	**YORKSHIRE AND LINCOLNSHIRE**	**2,125**
21	Yorkshire	1,822
22	Lincolnshire	303
3	**EAST MIDLANDS**	**1,283**
31	Derbyshire	247
32	Leicestershire	407
33	Northamptonshire	255
34	Rutland	1
35	Nottinghamshire	373
4	**EAST ANGLIA**	**515**
41	Cambridgeshire	124
42	Huntingdonshire	33
43	Norfolk	175
44	Suffolk	183
5	**SOUTH EAST**	**5,559**
51	Bedfordshire	290
52	Berkshire	360
53	Buckinghamshire	434
54	Essex	751
55	Hampshire	692
56	Hertfordshire	719
57	Kent	628
58	Surrey	1,036
585	Oxfordshire	180
59	Sussex	489
6	**SOUTH WEST**	**1,444**
61	Cornwall	97
62	Devonshire	261
63	Dorset	151
64	Gloucestershire	538
65	Somerset	206
66	Wiltshire	191
7	**WEST MIDLANDS AND WALES**	**3,426**
71	Herefordshire	41
72	Shropshire	71
73	Staffordshire	873
74	Warwickshire	1,320
75	Worcestershire	350
79	Wales	771
8	**NORTH WEST**	**2,880**
81	Cheshire	555
82	Lancashire	2,316
83	Isle of Man	9
9	**GREATER LONDON AND MIDDLESEX**	**6,665**
90	GLC	5,603
91	Middlesex	1,062
01	**NORTHERN IRELAND**	**319**
02	**EIRE**	**407**
		26,910
03	**OVERSEAS**	**98**
		Total 27,008

**When planning your programme
use the code number for easy reference.**

INDUSTRIES
(Standard Industrial Classifications)

CODE

A	Agriculture, Forestry, Fishing	46
B	Mining & Quarrying	77
C	Food, Drink & Tobacco	1,577
D	Coal & Petroleum Products	123
E	Chemicals & Allied Industries	1,254
F	Metal Manufacture	1,030
G	Mechanical Engineering	4,859
H	Instrument Engineering	427
I	Electrical Engineering	3,262
J	Shipbuilding & Marine Engineering	212
K	Vehicles	660
L	Metal Goods not elsewhere specified	1,316
M	Textiles	112
N	Leather, Leather Goods & Fur	291
O	Clothing & Footwear	171
P	Bricks, Pottery, Glass, Cement, etc.	530
Q	Timber, Furniture, etc.	312
R	Paper, Printing & Publishing	2,124
S	Other Manufacturing Industries	272
T	Construction	109
U	Gas, Electricity & Water	79
V	Transport & Communications	614
W	Distributive Trades	475
X	Insurance, Banking, Finance & Business Services	1,494
Y	Professional & Scientific Services	1,051
Z	Miscellaneous Services	1,600
ZZ	Public Administration & Defence	2,931
	Total	27,008

**When planning your programme
use the code letter for easy reference.**

MANAGEMENT STATUS

CODE

Admin.	Administration	12,269
O & M	O & M/Planning/Development	2,012
Prod.	Production	1,201
DP	Data Processing/Scientific/Technical	3,441
SM	Sales/Marketing	1,097
Pur.	Purchasing/Stock Control	1,284
Con.	Consultancy	285
Fin.	Financial	3,555
Govt.	Government	574
LL	Librarians/Lecturers etc.	723
		26,441
	Not specified	567
	Total	27,008

**When planning your programme,
use the code abbreviation for easy
reference.**

ABC
MEMBER OF THE AUDIT
BUREAU OF CIRCULATIONS

Audited circulation
January to December 1969 27,008

Markets Analysis

Fig. 3b   Source: Business Systems — Equipment Target Mailing Service

Figure 3.5   Penetration of sales outlets
In any one area at any one time the total number of outlets can vary. Some large companies can, over a period of time, develop a near monopoly situation in a region or town and force the closure of many smaller outlets. The significance of this development tends to restrict the number of opportunities which a company has available, for, if there are a large number of outlets, a salesman should be able to convert a number of prospects whereas, with one large outlet, the opportunity is severely limited. Sometimes industries go through a period of considerable rationalisation and the total number of outlets diminishes substantially. Once such a trend becomes apparent, it is vital that the company establishes the extent to which outlets it serves are declining in total compared to the national picture, in case its own outlets are closing at a greater rate than those of competitors.

Figure 3c   Size of outlets. In this illustration it is possible to use this basic information to note the extent to which each company is increasing its number of outlets by opening new accounts and retaining the business of established accounts. The system can also be used to prepare arbitrarily market shares by region and so have a guide to performance against that of competitors.

Figure 3.6   Competitive pricing chart
Because of the significance of pricing practices in any business environment it is necessary for every business to maintain surveillance over variations in the pricing strategy adopted from time to time by different companies.

In the chart illustrated it is possible to establish the effect of pricing strategy on each company's performance by product group and market share. Used properly, this chart can give indications of the price level at which maximum penetration may be achieved for any given product group.

FIGURE 3.5																	
DATE:		PENETRATION OF SALES OUTLETS										PREPARED BY:					
		Northern	Yorkshire & Humberside	East Anglia	South East	G.L.C.	South West	Wales	North West	Scotland	Northern Ireland	Total Homemarket	Overseas Area A	Overseas Area B	Overseas Area C	Total Overseas	Total Sales
Total Number of Outlets																	
Movement Prior Year																	
Sales Value from Outlets																	
Movement Prior Year																	
COMPANY A	active a/cs																
	% total																
	value £																
	% total																
	movement																
COMPANY B																	
COMPANY C																	
COMPANY D																	
COMPANY E																	

Figure 3c		Size of Outlets			
	Establishments	Enterprises	£m Net Output	£000's Net Output Per Establishment	£m Capital Expenditure
EMPLOYEES					
1 – 24					
25 – 99					
100 – 499					
500 – 1999					
2000 – 4999					
5000 – 9999					
10,000 – 19,999					
20,000 +					
All Manufacturing					

FIGURE 3.6

COMPETITIVE PRICING CHART

DATE:

PREPARED BY:

	sales	over + 15%	+ 15%	+15%	+12½%	+ 10%	+7½%	+ 5%	par price	– 5%	– 7½%	– 10%	– 12½%	over – 15%
Total Market Sales £														
Total Market Sales %	100													
Company A Product Group 1£														
Market Share %														
Product Group 2£														
Market Share %														
Product Group3 £														
Market Share %														
Product Group 4£														
Market Share %														
/////////////														
Company B Product Group 1£														
Market Share %														
Product Group 2 £														
Market Share %														
Product Group 3 £														
Market Share %														
Product Group 4£														
Market Share %														
Company B Product Group 1£														
Market Share %														
Product Group 2£														
Market Share %														
Product Group 3£														
Market Share %														
Product Group 4£														
Market Share %														

Analysis of Market Shares 4

In a competitive commercial environment the only certain way to monitor company performance is by comparison of results against those of competitors. The standards established in the appraisal of competitor profiles provide the foundation for a full analysis of market shares. Companies wishing to enter a market which is new to them will need to assess the extent to which policies adopted by present suppliers have been successful. In obtaining full information on the total market size it is necessary to assess the extent to which the market can be penetrated either by winning a share of the existing market or by concentrating on growth and winning the business which would normally have been obtained by the present suppliers.

Once these assessments have been made it is possible for the company to make a full and realistic evaluation of the marketing budget which will be required to achieve the planned penetration. In some industries winning business from established suppliers may be easier to achieve than expanding the total market. In other industries development of the growth potential may be more feasible than a battle against established suppliers to win business.

Measurement of the total market should be undertaken only after the business activity of the company has been determined and a reasoned definition of the total market prepared. There is frequent confusion about the total market for a particular product. It is, in fact, the total amount of money spent in the satisfaction of a need, irrespective of the products, which satisfy that need. This means all types of food compete against each other; the many different types of transport are competitors; all aids to business efficiency are in competition. The manufacturer who supplies only one kind of product to satisfy a need has a market by penetration, in which similar products compete directly against each other. A marketing-orientated company will not only win business from competitors for similar products but will also expand the market by penetration at the expense of indirect competitors for the total market.

The market situation for any company or industry is constantly changing and can experience violent fluctuations in market shares from day to day. Over a period of time there will be shifts in the pattern of demand and a company must keep constant track of such trends. A steadily rising sales turnover will not, by itself, indicate whether a firm is making best use of its potential. A company may have a reasonable increase in sales each year and yet still have a rapidly diminishing market share. Unless sales volume is rising at a rate not less than that of the industry as a whole, it will be losing sales opportunities.

In a rapidly expanding economy a depression will leave such companies in a very weak position against stronger competitors which have maintained surveillance on market trends. It is also essential for a company to keep track of the market shares for each of its major competitors and to be able to explain any change becoming apparent. If a competitor is expanding its market share at a greater rate than could be expected, there must be an explanation. The cause must be established quickly before the investigating company's own performance is affected by the expanding competitor. If, however, a major competitor which is known to be strong in its marketing activities begins to show a deterioration in market share, it is possible that the company had decided to diversify out of that market, either because it has forecast a decreasing rate of growth or because it has anticipated an increase in supply over demand, and the consequent marketing expense will not bring in the required profit performance. For these reasons it is vital for companies to carry out market share analysis on a continuous basis. It is usually better to carry out inexpensive elementary research at regular periods than to carry out extensive research projects infrequently.

Marketing research is frequently confused with market research. Marketing research is an activity which examines all the elements in marketing practice, including markets, products, distribution channels, pricing behaviour and opinions. Market research is just one element of marketing research, although easily the most widely known and practised. Today the average size of firms is increasing and business decisions are becoming even more critical. Not only are the financial consequences of each business decision becoming greater but the time span between decisions and the consequences is widening. Research into the distributive system will not necessarily determine the future but it can be used to illuminate the scene, eliminate the unlikely and spotlight the probable. It is an aid to reducing business risk.

Although the market research industry is growing rapidly, there are still relatively few firms which spend money in an effort to discover what is happening in the market-place. Research by manufacturers selling to the general public is more usual than it is with companies selling to industrial markets.

Some manufacturers of fast-moving consumer lines subscribe to continuous research carried out by retail audit investigators. By carrying out regular stock checks among a representative sample of retailers and calculating the quantity of goods sold by brand, the research company is able to appraise the market shares of leading companies and make this information available to its sub-

FIGURE 4-1

MARKET SHARES ANALYSIS - BY VALUE AND PRODUCT GROUP

DATE: PREPARED BY:

Prior Yr 1		Prior Yr 1		Company	Budget Yr		Plan Yr 1		Plan Yr 2		Plan Yr 3		Plan Yr 4		Plan Yr 5	
value	growth	value	growth	Major Product Group	value	growth	value	growth	value	growth	value	growth	value	growth	value	growth
				Product Group A												
				Product Group B												
				Product Group C												
				Product Group D												
				Total All Groups												
				Product Group A												
				Product Group B												
				Product Group C												
				Product Group D												
				Total All Groups												
				Product Group A												
				Product Group B												
				Product Group C												
				Product Group D												
				Total All Groups												
				Product Group A												
				Product Group B												
				Product Group C												
				Product Group D												
				Total All Groups												
				Product Group A												
				Product Group B												
				Product Group C												
				Product Group D												
				Total All Groups												
				Total Product Group A												
				Total Product Group B												
				Total Product Group C												
				Total Product Group D												
				Total All Product Groups												

FIGURE 4.2

MARKET SHARES ANALYSIS – BY VOLUME AND PRODUCT GROUP

DATE: PREPARED BY:

Prior Yr 1		Prior Yr 2		Company	Budget Yr		Plan Yr 1		Plan Yr 2		Plan Yr 3		Plan Yr 4		Plan Yr 5	
volume	growth	volume	growth	Major Product Group	volume	growth	volume	growth	volume	growth	volume	growth	volume	growth	volume	growth
				Product Group A												
				Product Group B												
				Product Group C												
				Product Group D												
				Total All Groups												
				Product Group A												
				Product Group B												
				Product Group C												
				Product Group D												
				Total All Groups												
				Product Group A												
				Product Group B												
				Product Group C												
				Product Group D												
				Total All Groups												
				Product Group A												
				Product Group B												
				Product Group C												
				Product Group D												
				Total All Groups												
				Product Group A												
				Product Group B												
				Product Group C												
				Product Group D												
				Total All Groups												
				Total Product Group A												
				Total Product Group B												
				Total Product Group C												
				Total Product Group D												
				Total Product Groups												

scribers. In the industrial field multi-client projects are gaining in popularity and have proved invaluable to the sponsors. A service provided for both consumer companies and industrial companies is the collection and analysis of detailed financial information which enables the businessman to compare his company's total performance against the industrial average. Although competitors are not identified by name, it is possible to relate the information supplied to other published information and to make direct comparisons.

Many business decisions are made which could have been supported or, perhaps, invalidated by the study of published information. Executives should be familiar with the many official publications and the information supplied by such bodies as trade associations, banks, chambers of commerce, embassies, national and local newspapers, the trade and technical press and the many directories which are published regularly. A list of such sources is provided in Appendix 1.

One of the most comprehensive services provided for industry by the Department of Trade and Industry is the Statistics and Marketing Intelligence Library. Freely available for public use is a collection of trade and other economic statistics, trade directories and manufacturers' catalogues, which can be consulted either by personal visit or by telephone or telex. Though the main purpose of the library is to provide a service in the field of foreign economic statistics, it also holds complete sets of all principal series of United Kingdom economic statistics.

The Companies Act 1967 has made it possible for an investigator to obtain substantial financial information on competitors. The formerly exempt private company no longer exists, such companies are now compelled by law to file an annual return, including a profit and loss account and a balance sheet. Such information about companies is readily available from Companies' House, London.

Figure 4.1 Market shares analysis by value and product group
This form makes provision for the detailed analysis of the investigating company by major product groups as well as its four major competitors. The total market penetration for each of the four major product groups and the total for all major product groups are shown at the end. This form also shows the performance of two previous years by actual value where known and the growth rate. It also shows the current year and the forward five years. In each case the sales value of each product group is shown as the growth rate over the previous year in percentage form. As an integral part of the marketing plan it will be necessary for the executive responsible for preparing this form to explain and justify the forecast growth for each major company shown. Normally the fifth section of the

form will be used for the total combined performance of the least significant competitors in the market.

Figure 4.2   Market shares analysis by volume and product group
This form differs from Figure 4.1 in that it provides information on physical units and will show growth rate according to actual production of goods. Not only does this form enable the investigator to make realistic forecasts irrespective of inflation, but it will enable him to include growth by competitors as a direct result of charging premium prices, or growth as a direct result of price cutting when Figures 4.1 and 4.2 are compared.

Figure 4a   Sales growth/sales strength ratios. Using this chart it is possible to compare sales strength with sales growth and any consistency between the two.

Figure 4.3   Market shares analysis by value and standard industrial classification
The number of industries which can be listed under these standard industrial classifications is almost limitless. The choice of industries will vary according to those significant to the individual company and there may not be as many as those provided for on this illustration. This form is particularly important to the company selling products across a broad range of industry and commerce. It will enable the company's management to assess which industries are growing and which declining and will, therefore, give a clear indication of where the salesmen's efforts should be concentrated and at which industries promotional activities should be devoted.

Frequently a product will serve a different purpose in a different industry. Specific marketing activity should be developed to exploit specific industries. Where this is necessary the company must carry out sufficient research to measure the effectiveness of competitors by way of penetration into these particular industries. Sometimes companies specialise within certain industries and can achieve a strong foothold because of the expertise they have gathered, either over a number of years or by a particular recruitment policy. To diversify into that industry against a strong competitor, it may be advisable for a company to recruit a specialist sales force with industry experience and knowledge.

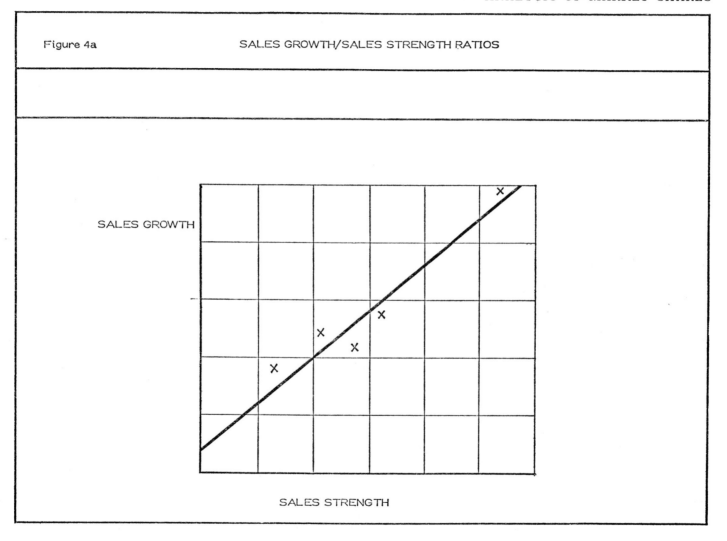

Figure 4a — SALES GROWTH/SALES STRENGTH RATIOS

SALES GROWTH

SALES STRENGTH

E

FIGURE 4,3

MARKET SHARES ANALYSIS – VALUE & STANDARD INDUSTRIAL CLASSIFICATION

DATE: PREPARED BY:

Prior Yr 1		Prior Yr 1		S.I.C.	Budget Yr		Plan Yr 1		Plan Yr 2		Plan Yr 3		Plan Yr 4		Plan Yr 5	
value	growth	value	growth		value	growth	value	growth	value	growth	value	growth	value	growth	value	growth
				1.												
				2.												
				3.												
				4.												
				5.												
				6.												
				7.												
				8.												
				9.												
				10.												
				11.												
				12.												
				13.												
				14.												
				15.												
				16.												
				17.												
				18.												
				19.												
				20.												
				21.												
				22.												
				23.												
				24.												
				25.												
				26.												

Figure 4.4 Market shares analysis by volume and standard industrial classification

Penetration into one particular industry may be achieved by pricing promotion and adjustment to normal company level once a strong foothold is established. This form of promotion may be strategic, in that the company intends to expand the market within a particular industry, or tactical, in that the company wishes to expand its own share of that industry at the expense of competitors. By making forecasts of both value and volume the company can make a controlled marketing effort, ensuring that only a marginal part of its production is committed to selling at lower than normal profit return ratios. By charting this operation over a period of seven or eight years the planner should give a clear indication about when the required volume is likely to be achieved; that is the point at which the swing towards full pricing will be indicated.

Figure 4.5 Market shares analysis by value and size of outlet

Over the past few years there has been a steady increase in the average size of firm from the very small retail outlet through all industries up to the larger industrial empires. At the same time there has been steady merging among non-competing companies, giving rise to the term "conglomerate company." This expression describes a large group of companies with diverse products and markets. It is reasonable to assume that this tendency is occurring more rapidly in some industries than in others. In industries where it is particularly marked, suppliers may be facing an increased marketing problem. With a reduction in the total potential outlets and with the buying strength of those remaining becoming more pronounced, suppliers become faced with increasing competition from suppliers experiencing a serious deterioration in profitability. By carefully assessing and watching closely the tendency towards such rationalisation among customers, the businessman is able to prepare for the consequences of such events. He may find it prudent to find outlets by acquiring competitors or by diversifying into other markets. In this illustration markets have been segmented carefully so a trend can be isolated and, where significant, more detailed investigation carried out into the actual industry concerned and also where possible into the geographical area which has already been significantly affected.

There are several different methods by which the size of the firm can be determined. It may be by sales turnover, or by capital employed, or by number of employees. The most reliable guide to size is probably that of number of employees and the categories provided are the groupings which can be extracted from the Census of Production.

Figure 4.6   Market shares analysis by volume and size of outlet

Where rationalisation has already begun it should be possible to establish to what extent it has affected prices by comparing volume in physical units against sales value and producing an average selling price per unit sold. It will also indicate whether rationalisation within industrial groupings is causing an increase in growth rate compared with other industrial segments.

These charts will also show the growth rate by size of outlet and indicate profitability by outlet size. The information produced should enable the company to embark upon a policy of selective selling. A decline in the number and the value of a particular size of outlet, if investigated and proved to be consistent with national performance, will provide guidance to the sales manager in directing the efforts and calling pattern of his sales personnel.

FIGURE 4.4

MARKET SHARES ANALYSIS - VOLUME AND STANDARD INDUSTRIAL CLASSIFICATION

DATE:

PREPARED BY:

Prior Yr 1		Prior Yr 1		S.I.C.	Budget Yr		Plan Yr 1		Plan Yr 2		Plan Yr 3		Plan Yr 4		Plan Yr 5	
volume	growth	volume	growth		volume	growth	volume	growth	volume	growth	volume	growth	volume	growth	volume	growth
				1.												
				2.												
				3.												
				4.												
				5.												
				6.												
				7.												
				8.												
				9.												
				10.												
				11.												
				12.												
				13.												
				14.												
				15.												
				16.												
				17.												
				18.												
				19.												
				20.												
				21.												
				22.												
				23.												
				24.												
				25.												
				26.												

FIGURE 4.5
DATE: MARKET SHARES ANALYSIS – VALUE AND SIZE OF OUTLET   PREPARED BY:

| Prior Yr 1 | | Prior Yr 1 | | Size of Outlet | Budget Yr | | Plan Yr 1 | | Plan Yr 2 | | Plan Yr 3 | | Plan Yr 4 | | Plan Yr 5 | |
value	growth	value	growth		value	growth	value	growth	value	growth	value	growth	value	growth	value	growth
				Manufacturing 0 – 25												
				26 – 50												
				51 – 100												
				101 – 250												
				251 – 500												
				501 – 1000												
				Over 1000												
				Total												
				Service 0 – 25												
				26 – 50												
				51 – 100												
				101 – 250												
				251 – 500												
				501 – 1000												
				Over 1000												
				Total												
				Distributive 0 – 25												
				26 – 50												
				51 – 100												
				101 – 250												
				251 – 500												
				501 – 1000												
				Over 1000												
				Total												
				Finance – Credit 0 – 25												
				26 – 50												
				51 – 100												
				101 – 250												
				251 – 500												
				501 – 1000												
				Over 1000												
				Total												

FIGURE 4.6   MARKET SHARES ANALYSIS – VOLUME AND SIZE OF OUTLET

DATE :   PREPARED BY:

Prior Yr 1		Prior Yr 1		Size of Outlet	Budget Yr		Plan Yr 1		Plan Yr 2		Plan Yr 3		Plan Yr 4		Plan Yr 5	
volume	growth	volume	growth		volume	growth	volume	growth	volume	growth	volume	growth	volume	growth	volume	growth
				Manufacturing 0 – 25												
				26 – 50												
				51 – 100												
				101 – 250												
				251 – 500												
				501 – 1000												
				Over 1000												
				Total												
				Service 0 – 25												
				26 – 50												
				51 – 100												
				101 – 250												
				251 – 500												
				501 – 1000												
				Over 1000												
				Total												
				Distributive 0 – 25												
				26 – 50												
				51 – 100												
				101 – 250												
				251 – 500												
				501 – 1000												
				Over 1000												
				Total												
				Finance – Credit 0 –25												
				26 – 50												
				51 – 100												
				101 – 250												
				251 – 500												
				501 – 1000												
				Over 1000												
				Total												

5 Control of Distribution

The deliberate selection of customers and the means by which they are served is an essential part of marketing strategy. In a marketing-orientated company, products have been developed for which sufficient market demand has been established. In measuring the market demand the company should have developed ideally a profile of a typical customer; all outlets which are close to matching that profile will be the target for the company's sales force, and for all other promotional activity. The manufacturer is concerned with ensuring that these customers are supplied with each product either by the development of appropriate channels of distribution or by delivering the product direct from his own warehouse or factory.

The distributive process has two essential elements. The channels of distribution are the means by which a product is promoted and sales progressed from manufacturer to ultimate consumer. Physical distribution is the actual transportation of goods from the point of origin to the point of actual consumption.

Channels of distribution in the consumer field have undergone considerable change in recent years. Apart from an immense increase in the numbers of supermarkets and self-service stores, some companies have achieved rapid growth by the provision of mail order facilities, while others have increased their market share by party plan selling methods.

Direct selling continues to grow and the use of franchise marketing methods is still considered to be a new concept with high growth potential. In the industrial field changes in distributive channels have not yet been significant but some have already become well established, leasing for factories and capital equipment and, more specifically, the use of computer bureaux for data processing. It is not only in the service field that progress can be made; the opportunities for alternatives are immense.

The cost to the nation of distribution became fully recognised when the government of the day introduced a tax on services of which the distribution process is perhaps the most significant. Certainly the cost to industry of distributing a product may range from 15 to 60 per cent of the ultimate selling price, according to the nature of the product and the distribution channels chosen. Active control of distribution can reduce these costs and allow a substantial increase in profitability.

Apart from the actual direct costs incurred, many related functions could be improved in effectiveness following the improvement of actual distribution. For example, a study of the levels of geographical market demand and of purchasing patterns, by day of the week or time of the year, enables a supplier to arrange effective stock control at each warehouse point and then to plan entire production schedules according to forecast demand. Distribution is a critical part of marketing management and is the means by which a company can increase its sales volume and its own profitability. The distribution process is essential to provide for customers' needs with the right product at the right time at the right place at the right price.

The marketing executive must endeavour to reconcile the needs of customers for a full service with the needs of his own company to provide a minimum level of service. If he should decide that the most appropriate means by which his company can win sales at the expense of competitors is by providing a distribution service superior to his competitors, then the cost of that service is a deliberate expense incurred in the marketing budget as an alternative to other marketing activities and expenditure.

Often, however, the manufacturer will endeavour to supply the maximum service at minimum cost. This usually means providing immediate delivery, relatively speaking, for products in frequent demand but an extended delivery for less popular products. In the consumer goods field supermarket chains measure the performance of an individual outlet by comparing its performance in growth against the average for a previous period of sales per square foot of floor space or per employee or even per customer. A ratio of scales of different operating costs are kept in addition to staff lists and details of absenteeism. These are additional to the traditional measurements of retail effectiveness, such as rate of stock turnover and net profit as a percentage of capital employed.

Because of the forces of competition, the demand for any one product from any one source and any one particular type can vary substantially. It is the distributive function to provide a contingency against such wide variations in demand, and the businessman's responsibility to develop a distributive pattern which will cater for these deviations from the norm. Some are predictable, and the product mix from the factory must be adjusted to meet demand. By developing a replenishment mean time, and progressing stocks through the channels of distribution while still maintaining a constant delivery pattern, the businessman is able to design a distributive system which will operate not only effectively but also economically. It must be remembered that carrying stocks is not only for the benefit of customers, it also serves the purpose of allowing the factory production to continue without frequent changes, according to day-to-day pressure on production facilities. Properly controlled, the distributive system can protect a company against giving customer dissatisfaction and will enable it to achieve a high level of productivity by ensuring economical production runs according to predetermined programming.

In recent years there has been a steady shift of emphasis in the consumer goods field from sales force selling to the creation of demand by advertising. This transition has been assisted by the increasing power of communications – the advent of commercial television and the boom in newspaper and periodical publishing, and also the breakdown in territorial boundaries between countries because of the increasing popularity of air travel and holidays abroad.

Companies supplying goods for consumption by the general public now stimulate selling by creating a demand by advertising and the use of merchandising techniques at point of sale. The silent salesman, as point of sale advertising is known, is a constant reminder of the product's existence and of the satisfaction it provides to the consumer. Merchandising techniques include the use of colour and design in the presentation of goods for sale. In the industrial field merchandising techniques cover all sales aids used to support salesmen when calling on customers or potential customers, and may include the use of films, videotapes, flip charts and sales manuals, as well as the more traditional specimen cases, samples and printed brochures.

Realising and justifying the need for new branch offices or warehouses is a project which is worth considerable time and effort by the businessman when the costs, both direct and indirect, are considered. An example is the continued use of a centralised office or warehouse when demand in another area is such that valuable profits are being lost because the company does not have the appropriate information on which to base a decision on the need for a new branch. Opening a new office and allowing the local salesman to work from that office does not normally require a substantial investment, but it does justify the appointment of a branch manager who will need to carry the full responsibility for the area's profitability. The new branch manager responsible for performance which has never previously been measured is faced with failure. No one has yet discovered a means of measuring something that does not exist. Simply believing that demand exists is insufficient.

Opening a new warehouse will always involve considerable expense and the businessman must ensure that the new warehouse is justified by a requirement for service at a sufficiently high volume which cannot be catered for adequately by the transportation of goods from the factory or by a reduction in transport charges using bulk transport facilities. Before considering a new warehouse the company should first evaluate every other means of providing the required facilities. Is it possible that service from the factory can be improved by an overhaul of the present system, perhaps by giving priority to the region under pressure, particularly if in other regions delivery is not quite so

FIGURE 5.1

DATE:

PHYSICAL DISTRIBUTION COSTS

PREPARED BY:

PRODUCT	Internal							External						Other Costs	Overseas	Control	
	Transfer Charges	Salaries & Wages	Interest	Movement	Warehousing	Wastage	Total	Vehicles	Interest	Wages	Wastage	Charges	Total		Shipping Insurance & Carriage	Total Costs	Costs per Unit

FIGURE 5.2

DISTRIBUTION COSTS COMPARISON

DATE:

PREPARED BY:

PRODUCT	ROAD				RAIL			SEA					AIR			POST					
	Own Transport	Contract Hire	Carriers	Other	Passenger	Freight	Other	In Bond	On Deck	Hold	Hovercraft	Other	Parcel	Freight	Other	1st Class	2nd Class	Parcel Post	Other	Waterways	Other

critical? There may also be faster means of transport which, though more expensive when compared with the regular means of distribution, may well be considerably less than the cost of opening a new warehouse. It may also be possible for a new warehouse to be opened as a satellite to a main warehouse which is closer than the factory and from which buffer stocks can be drawn as required. The location of branch offices and warehouses, and the selection and appointment of appropriately sited salesmen to ensure adequate distribution of the company's products are a vital part of the marketing process.

Figure 5.1 Physical distribution costs

Few companies appreciate fully the true extent to which physical distribution has grown as a proportion of the selling costs for a product. In this chart likely costs have been divided into those incurred internally within an organisation, and those which will be incurred in the actual carriage of the goods. Allowance is made for those goods which may be shipped overseas and for which the distribution costs will be greater than those sold on the home market.

On this chart all costs are compared by product as the costs of distribution per product often vary according to the value of the goods, their bulk or shape or the container used. Often, in analysing distribution costs in this way, the businessman discovers that some of his best-selling lines yield little or no profit but do make substantial contributions to overheads. By establishing this fact he knows where to concentrate his priorities should an opportunity arise for a bulk order which may fill up production capacity at the expense of more profitable opportunities.

Figure 5.2 Distribution costs comparison

This illustration is a guide on how best to fulfil customer requirements for urgent delivery and the cost of providing the service demanded. With a chart of this description readily available, the decision whether a particular consignment should be dispatched urgently by passenger train or by air parcel is a simple one. Often there is little to choose in terms of time in sending goods by passenger train or by air because of the comparative inflexibility of UK airports.

Of particular importance to the businessman is the guide shown in this document on whether the manufacturer wishes to be within the transport business himself, as well as being a manufacturer, or whether it would be advisable for him to leave it to the specialist distributors to provide an

FIGURE 5.3

DISTRIBUTION SERVICES AND CHARGES

DATE: PREPARED·BY:

Destination	Airline		Air Agent A			Air Agent B			Air Agent C			Air Agent D			Air Agent E		
	Kilo Rates	Minimum Charge	Kilo Rates	Minimum Charge	Departure Days	Kilo Rates	Minimum Charge	Departure Days	Kilo Rates	Minimum Charge	Departure Days	Kilo Rates	Minimum Charge	Departure Days	Kilo Rates	Minimum Charge	Departure Days

FIGURE 5.4

STOCK RECORD CARD

DATE: PREPARED BY:

ITEM	Ref. No.	Price	Maximum Stock	Minimum Stock	Re-order level	Date Received	Order Number	Received from or issued to	Quantity Received	Quantity issued	Quantity Missing	Balance Remaining	VALUE

adequate service to meet all his needs. In practice very few companies can justify their own transport fleets although the volume that these firms handle would seem to justify the expense incurred. Certainly no individual company could possibly afford to provide the full range of facilities which are available from specialist transport companies and services.

Figure 5.3 Distribution services and charges

Some manufacturers find it worth while to send a major proportion of their exported goods by air. Usually these commodities are small in size but high in value – for example, jewellery, works of art, drugs and essential oils. Many of these manufacturers use shipping or forwarding agents rather than setting up their own specialist department to handle the documentation and the administration involved. These agents may use scheduled airlines or may charter flights at periodic intervals. There can be considerable variation in their charges and the facilities they are able to offer.

Using this illustration the exporter is able to weigh the cost of different agents against the urgency of a particular consignment. Some agents provide first-class facilities for certain areas of the world in which they have built up a considerable volume of business and their charges may compare favourably with other agents for those areas. In other parts of the world they may suffer in comparison, their charges and facilities not being competitive. This illustration shows the exporter how to control his use of agents for certain areas and he is able to choose whichever agent provides him with the best service at the most competitive rates for a particular destination.

Figure 5.4 Stock record card

Different methods of stock valuation may have a favourable or adverse effect on a company's annual profit statement. A high valuation of stock will appear to inflate the net profit of the business, whereas a low valuation will produce a less than realistic net profit. It is essential that the actual value of stock held by the company is a realistic one and full control procedures must be introduced.

The stock which a company carries is a buffer against fluctuations in demand and is a pliable part of company marketing strategy. Stocks of slow-moving goods must be carried at the minimum level according to needs and it is usually better to manufacture in small quantities at a high unit cost rather than manufacture at normally economic levels and carry too high a stock. Stock ties up the company's working capital and uncontrolled stock levels can cause a serious deterioration in the

FIGURE 5.5.

BRANCH ORGANISATION – FIXED EXPENSES

DATE: PREPARED BY:

BRANCH	Rent	Rates	Insurance	Depreciation	Interest	Asst. Labour Benefits	Paid Holidays	Mgt. Headcount	Mgt. Salaries	Head count Sales force	Sales force Salaries	Headcount Clerks	Clerical Wages	Total Manpower	Total Fixed Expense

F

company's cash flow; a frequent cause of bankruptcy. Values in a proper stock control record with maximum, minimum and reorder stock levels, each determined as part of marketing policy, will help to ensure that the needs of customers are met, production programming is efficient and the company's resources are adequately employed.

Figure 5.5   Branch organisation, fixed expenses

A branch organisation must be viewed as an almost autonomous profit-making operation in its own right. There is no justification for any branch which does not perform its company function in producing maximum profits for the capital invested. The fixed expenses shown in this illustration are those items of expenditure which have to be recovered irrespective of sales handled by that branch. If accounted for in the manner shown, this chart will provide the basic information for the branch break-even point in sales volume. It will also be a guide to the expense which will be incurred should a new branch be opened in another region, and will also indicate the volume of sales to be obtained over and above those already being serviced direct from the factory. In opening a new branch, businessmen tend to think only of the sales volume already being obtained and that it alone will justify the opening of a branch.

What is not realised is that the present sales volume in a particular area is already contributing to present overheads at the factory and by opening a branch in the area additional costs are incurred which can only be paid for out of increased volume.

Figure 5.6   Branch organisation, variable expenses

Although the expenditure shown in this chart is subject to considerable variation, according to the volume of business and the administrative procedures necessary in obtaining and monitoring business, it is essential that every part is a budgeted expense and is subject to the control which becomes an integral part of branch organisation. Necessarily, every item is considered to be justified in practice in order to achieve branch objectives. All items listed are those which would normally be incurred in business; individual companies will be able to add those items which are peculiar to their own systems or procedures. When linked with Figure 5.5 the two charts provide the fundamental part of individual branch profit and loss statements and will be the basis for overall control.

FIGURE 5.6

BRANCH ORGANISATION – VARIABLE EXPENSES

DATE:

PREPARED BY:

BRANCH	Commissions	Labour Wages	Asst. Labour Benefits	Overtime	Welfare	Training	Lighting	Heating	Repairs & Maintenance	Stationery	Postage	Telephone	Publicity	Discounts	Miscellaneous	Total

6　Schedule of Publicity

Publicity is an integral part of the total marketing operation, not an isolated group of activities which do not conform to the principles of marketing method, appraisal and measurement. To be effective all forms of publicity must have clearly defined objectives aimed at achieving the total marketing policy of a company and be part of the marketing mix aimed at producing the required company profit. Taken in this context, the true purpose of advertising is to sell.

In some marketing operations, such as mail order, advertising is the largest single item in the marketing budget and its true relevance to selling is easily discernible. In many consumer goods industries the ratio of advertising to other marketing activities is high and its selling function readily appreciated. In the industrial field the impact of advertising cannot be recognised easily and attempts at measuring its effectiveness have not been significant. For this reason many businessmen tend to regard publicity as a luxury which can be afforded only during prosperous times. The publicity appropriation is considered to be the least important item during times of economic pressure. This action is justified by businessmen on the pretext that advertising is used to inform; to the modern marketing manager this is only a half truth.

Advertising as a communication is a means of informing, but, more appropriately, it is a means of informing in such a way as to persuade a prospect to consider actively a purchase from the advertiser. The visuals and the copy are deliberately aimed at emphasising the most favourable features of the product concerned, partly to inform, but mainly to persuade.

In a free society advertising has a vital part to play in increasing the standard of living of the population. In a society where products are created to satisfy a known and measured need, the information process emphasising the benefits which consumers can derive from a purchase helps to create a mass market, so reducing the unit price of the product. At the time of the launch when the selling price has been determined, the company will have forecast the volume of sales expected, based on a measured demand at a given price level. Without advertising, the company marketing such a product would have to rely upon word of mouth and many years may pass before the required volume and economic price can be achieved. The time-span may be such that the company may be forced to charge a premium price in order to recover its investment, so making the purchase price too high for the majority of people who could have used and enjoyed the product. By stimulating demand with publicity, every company is contributing towards a higher level of employment by

TABLE 3 (a)

READERSHIP OF DAILY NEWSPAPERS ANALYSED WITHIN MAJOR RESPONSIBILITIES (Q.8)

UNIVERSE - ALL (£2,000+)

	TOTAL	Gen. Mangt.	Trspt.	Prd./ Eng.	Mkt./ Sales Hm.	Mkt./ Sales Ov.	Fin. Acct.	Persnl.	Rsch. & Dev.	Purch.	Co. Law/ Co. Sec.	Off. Mangt.	Other
UNWEIGHTED BASE	1000	455	75	115	190	74	166	212	80	107	81	114	175
	%	%	%	%	%	%	%	%	%	%	%	%	%
FINANCIAL TIMES	34	34	22	32	39	39	40	25	21	47	51	32	36
THE TIMES	23	28	33	33	26	27	20	16	27	34	13	21	25
TIMES NEWS SECTION	22	27	33	34	26	27	20	16	26	34	13	21	23
TIMES BUSINESS NEWS	21	26	33	29	25	24	20	15	21	29	17	18	25
THE GUARDIAN	11	12	9	16	7	8	11	13	6	9	25	16	10
DAILY TELEGRAPH	45	38	25	43	56	55	40	51	49	36	35	45	52
DAILY MAIL	29	31	29	28	29	34	28	26	14	26	26	33	34
DAILY EXPRESS	32	37	39	32	31	28	43	28	22	33	38	37	30

Figure 6a

Source: Reading Habits of British Businessmen
Financial Times/Observer/Opinion Research Centre 1970

LONDON MONDAY

BBC2 PROGRAMMES (TVR, %share TVR ITV BBC2)

BBC1 PROGRAMMES

Minute-by-minute TVR
100% = 4,270,000 HOMES
LONDON MON 30 NOV 70

ITV PROGRAMMES

QUARTER HOUR by QUARTER HOUR

providing jobs for workers and by ensuring a satisfactory return for those seeking an income from their investments.

The advertising world of today offers such a broad range of promotional services that its activities are now more appropriately called publicity services. Advertising agents now offer marketing research activities as well as specialist departments devoted to public relations, direct mail, promotional film production, design and production of sales promotion literature and press-cutting services. The role of the advertising agent in the future will continue to change as will the total concept of advertising, particularly in its approach to company problems.

Historically, advertising has been used as a means of stimulating increased sales volume. With an increase in the standard of education, combined with increasing company size, an advertising approach will be developed towards the protection of market shares, avoiding the erosion in profit which comes from overemphasis on pricing tactics in marketing practice. In addition, advertising strategy will be developed in such a way that it will become easier to concentrate the approach on predetermined consumer or industrial groupings. By concentrating strategy on individual groups it is possible to generate more specific, and, therefore, more compelling benefits where characteristics or needs tend to be similar.

In future years, publicity expenditure will become increasingly subject to scientific methods of measurement for effectiveness. While it is still not possible to measure the exact contribution advertising makes to sales volume, it is possible to measure the effectiveness of the objectives of advertising, and publicity in any form, as an investment of company resources. Advertising expenditure must be justified in the same way as any other form of investment. The pattern of advertising campaigns in the future will be divided into specific and logical steps. It will be necessary to define specific advertising objectives. The company must choose the message to be communicated to its markets in order to achieve the predetermined objectives. Copy, layout and even impact of advertisements must be pretested before the appropriation is committed to their use. More emphasis is likely in the projection of media in terms of cost effectiveness through coverage and opportunity to see by the selected audience most appropriate to the advertiser. The effectiveness of the total campaign can then be measured by comparing actual results with the original objectives.

Several specialist companies provide much valuable information for advertisers. The National Readership Survey and the detailed analysis carried out by the Opinion Research Centre (*Figure 6a*) are essential for press media selection. Audits of Great Britain Limited (*Figure 6b*) provide detailed analyses of television viewing while the Legion Publishing Company (*Figures 6c and 6d*) provide

Figure 6c

PRODUCT or SERVICE	AGENT	PND	QND	PNS	QNS	LOS	WWK	WMO	GWK	GMO	PRO	T&T	PRESS	TV	TOTAL
A.C.M. CALCULATORS	HAND	-	375	-	-	-	-	-	-	-	214	529	1116	-	1116
ASCOTA ACCOUNTING MACHINES	OATL	-	-	-	-	-	-	-	-	-	-	335	335	-	335
B.C.M. MULTI-SUSIE COMPUTER	STNO	-	-	-	-	-	-	-	-	-	-	433	433	-	433
BROUGHTON CALCULATOR	CCMP	-	187	-	-	-	-	-	-	-	-	-	187	-	187
BURROUGHS COMPUTER SYSTEM	AAMW	-	-	-	2675	-	-	-	-	-	-	-	2675	-	2675
CZ SCENTRON ACCTNG MACHINES	OATL	-	-	-	-	-	-	-	-	-	-	500	500	-	500
CASIO ELECTRONIC CALCULATOR	STNO	-	-	-	-	-	-	-	-	-	-	255	255	-	255
DECIMO CASH REGISTER	ROSM	-	-	-	-	-	-	-	-	-	-	60	60	-	60
DEKON CALCULATOR	STNO	-	-	-	-	-	-	-	-	-	-	442	442	-	442
ELECTRONIC ASSOC COMPUTERS	ALHA	-	-	-	-	-	-	-	-	-	-	300	300	-	300
ELLAMS UNITREX ADDING MACHINE	FEAN	-	-	-	-	-	-	-	-	-	-	122	122	-	122
FRIDEN ELECTRONIC CALCULATOR	DT&V	-	2112	-	-	-	-	-	-	-	-	-	2112	-	2112
G.E.I.S. COMPUTERS	BESS	-	-	-	-	-	-	-	-	-	80	-	80	-	80
HONEYWELL COMPUTERS	PARS	-	-	-	-	-	-	-	-	-	297	265	562	-	562
IBM UK COMPUTERS	B&B	-	4927	-	2080	-	-	-	340	-	-	300	7647	-	7647
ICL COMPUTERS	BENS	-	-	-	-	-	-	-	680	-	-	1120	1800	-	1800
KIENZLE ACCOUNTING MACHINES	BRHA	-	-	-	-	-	-	-	-	-	-	80	80	-	80
NCR ACCOUNTING MACHINES	INLK	-	-	-	-	-	-	-	-	-	-	645	645	-	645
NCR CASH REGISTER	INLK	-	-	-	-	-	-	-	-	-	-	570	570	-	570
NCR COMPUTERS	INLK	-	3285	-	5632	-	-	-	-	-	420	1486	10823	-	10823
NCR - PRESTIGE RANGE	INLK	-	-	-	-	-	-	-	-	-	157	-	157	-	157
OEM ADDING/LISTING MACHINES	ROSC	-	-	-	-	-	-	-	-	-	-	240	240	-	240
OLIVETTI CALCULATORS	PKL	-	-	-	-	-	-	-	1115	-	1058	-	2173	-	2173
OLYMPIA ADDING MACHINES	DORL	-	-	-	-	-	-	-	-	-	-	85	85	-	85
OLYMPIA CALCULATORS RANGE	DORL	-	285	-	-	-	-	-	-	-	-	680	965	-	965
PETCO CASH TILL	STEP	-	-	-	-	-	-	-	-	-	-	11	11	-	11
PHILIPS ELECTRIC CALCULATOR	WFWQ	-	1003	-	-	-	-	-	-	-	-	645	1648	-	1648
PHILIPS OFFICE COMPUTER	WFWQ	-	660	-	-	-	-	-	340	-	-	510	1510	-	1510
SADIE & SUSIE COMPUTERS	STNO	-	-	-	-	-	-	-	-	-	-	270	270	-	270
SHARP CALCULATOR	OSPE	1440	-	-	-	-	-	-	-	-	-	510	1950	-	1950
SHILOCK CALCULATORS	ALHA	-	340	-	-	-	-	-	-	-	-	876	1216	-	1216
UNIVAC COMPUTERS	OATL	-	528	-	-	-	-	-	-	-	73	592	1193	-	1193
VICTOR ADDING MACHINES	-	-	-	-	-	-	-	-	-	-	-	302	302	-	302
WANG CALCULATORS	-	-	-	-	-	-	-	-	-	-	-	140	140	-	140
TOTAL		1440	13702	-	10387	-	-	-	2475	-	2299	12303	42606	-	42606

PTVA-7

Source: Legion Publishing Company

Figure 6d

MG	MEDIA	DY	DT	D/T	SIZE/DUR	£	MG	MEDIA	DY	DT	D/T	SIZE/DUR	£	MG	MEDIA	DY	DT	D/T	SIZE/DUR	£
	A.D.M. CALCULATORS							DECIMO CASH REGISTER						QND	Finan Times	Th	20		13x5	730
																Th	27		15x5	900
QND	Finan Times	We	12	X	10x3	375	T&T	Chem&Drug	Sa	29		½p	32		Guardian	Th	20		13x5	552
								Grocer	Sa	1	SUP	4x2	28		Times	Th	20	X	"	1120
PRO	Bhm Post	Th	13		10x3	68														
	Leeds YP	Th	13		"	86		DENON CALCULATOR						QNS	Sun Times	Su	23		13x5	2080
	Ipl D Post	Th	13		"	60														
							T&T	Bus Eq Dig		Au		½p	140	GWK	Economist	Sa	22		1p	340
T&T	Bus Eq Dig		Au		1p	270		Index		Au		"	180							
	Index		Au	2C	8x2	137		Office Eq News		Au		"	122	T&T	Director		Au	FM	1p	300
	Office Eq News		Au		½p	122														
														ICL	COMPUTERS					
	ASCOTA ACCOUNTING MACHINES							ELECTRONIC ASSOC COMPUTERS						GWK	Economist	Sa	8		1p	340
																Sa	22		"	340
T&T	Mgmt Action		Au	1FC	1p	95	T&T	Computer Wkly	Th	13		10x4	300							
	Office Eq News		Au		"	240									T&T	Business Adm		Au		1p	230
															Business Mgmt		Au	FM	"	140
	B.C.L. MULTI-SUSIE COMPUTER							ELLAMS UNITREX ADDING MCH							Director		Au	"	"	300
															Mgmt To-day		Au		"	450
T&T	Business Adm		Au	B	1p	253	T&T	Office Eq News		Au		½p	122							
	Index		Au		½p	180									KIENZLE ACCTNG MACHINES					
								FRIDEN ELECTRONIC CALCULATOR												
	BROUGHTON CALCULATOR						QND	Finan Times	We	5		1p	2112	T&T	Natl Bldr		Au		1p	80
QND	Guardian	Tu	11		11x2	187		G.E.I.S. COMPUTERS							NCR ACCOUNTING MACHINES					
	BURROUGHS COMPUTER SYSTEM						PRO	Bghtn E Arg	We	12	SUP	½p	80	T&T	Bus Eq Dig		Au		1p	270
															Index		Au		10x3\	135
QNS	Sun Times	Su	30		13x5	2675		HONEYWELL COMPUTERS							Office Eq News		Au		1p	240
	CZ SOEMTRON ACCTNG MACHINES						PRO	Belf Newsltr	Th	6	SUP	½p	297	NCR	CASH REGISTER					
T&T	Business Adm		Au		1p	230	T&T	Science Jnl		Au	FM	1p	265	T&T	Hardware TJ	Fr	14		1p	102
	Bus Eq Dig		Au		"	270									Pharma Jnl	Sa	15	BP	"	180
								IBM UK COMPUTERS							Retail Chem	Th	20		10x4	160
	CASIO ELECTRONIC CALCULATOR														Self Service	Th	13	FM	1p	128
T&T	Office Eq News		Au	B	1p	255		Dly Tele	Th	20		13x5	75							

PTVD-1

Source: Legion Publishing Company

comprehensive reports on advertising expenditure by individual companies in selected media grouped by industry. Some of the principal advertising media provide their own reading and noting studies (*Figure 6e*). Sometimes, in conjunction with advertisers, they provide information on response rates and, occasionally, conversion rates of inquiries into orders.

Pre-testing advertisements has been undertaken on a limited scale by exposing alternative campaigns to audiences, selected at random or by quota and judging their reaction to these trials —presupposing that the sample will be representative of the characteristics of the total market. While these tests are never likely to produce the stroke of genius that characterises the company that achieves rapid growth in a short period of time, they do tend to ensure that total failure is eliminated. For companies spending vast sums on advertising the cost of research may be so minimal that even a marginal increase in sales volume covers research expenditure.

To many businessmen the selection of an advertising agency presents one of the most difficult and critical tasks in ensuring their future prosperity. The justification for using an agency is simply the need for professional skill which would be uneconomic for the advertiser to obtain by recruiting the necessary staff, even if such staff were readily available. In hiring the services of an agency the businessman expects the agency to provide creative thinking, competent media knowledge, realistic commercial comprehension and an understanding of progressive and enlightened business attitudes. Although he may not require the full range of services the modern agency can provide, he will expect his agency to have experience of similar products, a broad experience of the market, other industries and products, initiative, speed and considerable enthusiasm for his own product. The illustrations shown in this chapter are designed to ensure that the businessman applies the principles of marketing planning to his publicity appropriation.

Figure 6.1   Appropriation analysis

The basis of this form is to relate the publicity function to achieving the objectives closely associated with the forecast sales volume. Budgeted expenditure covers the full-time span of the marketing period, and actual financial expenditure on publicity does not have to be correlated to forecast sales volume. Expenditure is to be devoted to the achievement of year-by-year objectives in terms of increasing market awareness of the company, its products, benefits, and the additional services provided which, within themselves, must be closely related to the industries which will be served. The geographical areas in which industries are located and within which the company plans to

No. of Occasions	London	Lancs	TWW	STH	Midland	TT	Average
0							
1							
2							
3							
4							
5							
6							
7							
8							
9							
10 +							
Average							

Figure 66 l

% OF TOTAL POPULATION SEEING ADVERTISEMENT A NUMBER OF TIMES

FIGURE 6.1

APPROPRIATION ANALYSIS

DATE:

PREPARED BY:

Prior Yr Actual		Current Yr Budget		Media	Plan Year One		Plan Year Two		Plan Year Three		Plan Year Four		Plan Year Five	
value	%	value	%		value	%	value	%	value	%	value	%	value	%
				Established Products										
				New Products										
				Total										
				National Dailies										
				National Sundays										
				London Evenings										
				Colour Supplements										
				Provincial Press										
				Consumer Magazines										
				Trade & Technical Press										
				Independent T.V.										
				Colour T.V.										
				Outdoor Advertising										
				Commercial Radio										
				Cinemas										
				Direct Mail										
				House to house distribution										
				Telephone directory. Y. pages										
				Bingo Hall Advertising										
				Agency Service Charge										
				Total										
				Public Relations Seminars										
				Exhibitions										
				Press										
				Fees										
				Total										
				Sales Promotional Literature										

achieve a greater degree of penetration than in the past must also be considered. In establishing its goals the company must decide whether its approach to advertising is to win new business at the expense of competitors, or whether it intends to expand the total market by penetration, by developing a unique selling proposition, so as to ensure brand loyalty from its customers. This form provides an analysis of expenditure on established products and on new products. It goes on to divide the appropriation between the available media. Ideally, for control purposes, each medium used and the money planned to be spent on each medium should be divided into established products and new lines. A product can be classified as new to the company for whatever period of time the company concerned chooses, but it is advisable to classify products as new until such time as development costs have been fully recovered and the product is making its planned contribution to profitability. This would not, normally, be longer than three years.

Few companies would normally use the full range of media listed but the form is recommended for use as shown as it provides a checklist of available media before the appropriation is finally settled. Justification for and against each medium should be prepared in line with the advertising objectives.

Figure 6.2 Appropriation schedule
This is a much simpler form and, apart from the two historical years, is a complete analysis of advertising cash flow for each month of the first year of the marketing plan. The businessman may choose for himself whether he divides each sub-heading by product, by geographical area or by specific publicity medium. Ideally, each schedule should be subdivided into customer applications—that is, the use to which customers actually employ a product to any significant degree in terms of value. Each of the applications can then be categorised into an established or new product.

Careful preparation of the schedule well in advance of the year concerned will ensure a satisfactory cash flow is provided for the benefit of the company's accounting procedures. By deciding well in advance at which time of the year the company plans to spend money on various forms of publicity, each must be related to some particular objective. Objectives may be related to other events, such as major exhibitions, special features being planned by the press, direct mail campaigns, premium promotions, or the launching of a new product (*Figure 6f*).

It is always advisable to allot a small contingency allowance in the appropriation to avoid inflexibility at a time of unusual events or occurrences which the company considers should be exploited at the time, rather than upset the planned schedule in any way. The danger of using this contingency allowance as a buffer for extravagance in progressing other planned promotions must be avoided. Use of the contingency fund should be subjected to the same justification, appraisal and measurement as other items in the budget.

The percentage growth section for each year is an indication of any increased expenditure through particular media but can also be used as a guide to increases in the rate card for some magazines or newspapers. This will, itself, justify an immediate investigation into the cost-effectiveness of that medium compared to others which may not have increased their rates to the same extent.

Figure 6.3   Production record

It is not unusual for advertisers and advertising agencies to lose track of the detailed administration necessary to programme advertising campaigns properly. Often, at the last possible moment, a publication will remind its client that blocks are required urgently and it is at this point that everyone has to abandon other pressing tasks temporarily, in order to gather together, hastily, people responsible for copy, visualising, artwork, photography and block-making. It is not surprising that campaigns developed in such a way tend to be ineffective. The only way in which this haphazard practice can be avoided is for each campaign to be planned well in advance with the individuals responsible clearly briefed and target dates set for work to be completed. Only by providing critical dates with properly recorded lead times for the preparation of material can full production and a progressing system be developed.

Each date can be carefully noted in the master record and a follow-up system introduced. The system recommended is the preparation of files numbered one to thirty-one with each number signifying the appropriate day of the month; each morning, before commencement of the day's activities, the documents for that particular day are extracted from the file and actioned as necessary. The master chart should be incorporated in the total marketing plan booklet, and, should any documents be required urgently, a check on the master record will indicate the date in the follow-up system to which the necessary documents relate.

Prior Year Actual	Current Yr Budget	Media	1	2	3	4	5	6	7	8	9	10	11	12
		Press												
		T.V.												
		Posters												
		Sales Promotion												
		Public Relations												
		Others												
		Totals												

FIGURE 6.2

APPROPRIATION SCHEDULE

DATE:

PREPARED BY:

ADVERTISING/BUSINESS SYSTEMS   MAILING/WEEKS   Figure 6f

	W/Page	W/Page (f/m)	2/3 Page	$\frac{1}{2}$ Page	$\frac{1}{2}$ Page (f/m)	Week 1	Week 2	Week 3	Week 4	Response	Conversion	Remarks
Jan												
Feb												
Mar												
Apr												
May												
Jun												
July												
Aug												
Sep												
Oct												
Nov												
Dec												
Cost						Source: Business Systems & Equipment Target Mailing Service						

Figure 6.4   Space records

Once a company starts to justify in detail its expenditure with any specific publication or medium, it often finds that its knowledge of the publication concerned is inadequate. Although the advertisement managers of publications are always willing to supply information and media planners of advertising agencies have much data available, the final responsibility for the selection of media must always rest with the executive in the company responsible for authorising money spent on advertising. It is not enough for the executive to plead that he relies upon the guidance of his agency, for some agencies will be biased towards their own vested interests as, in general, more money spent by their clients will mean a higher return for the agency concerned.

Agencies are also in business to make a profit and occasionally to the surprise of companies they recommend a higher level of expenditure than might be justified in the circumstances. In addition, media planners are visited by sales promotional executives from different publications, each of whom can produce plausible evidence that their publication will be more effective than others. To avoid such possibilities the company executive should develop his own records based upon his own requirements and insert the information available from reliable sources according to his own definitions, or, at least, according to definitions which are strictly comparable, so eliminating as much bias as possible. The record cards suggested in this illustration will help to ensure that unavoidable costs which may well be hidden in the information supplied are understood and agreed in advance. Much of the information contained within this suggested record card can be obtained from the publication *British Rate and Data*, the media planner's standard source of reference.

Figure 6.5   Space register

No matter how much information is obtainable about different publications, that information serves no useful purpose until it is analysed or used as a comparison against its counterparts. The common denominator of the advertising world is cost-effectiveness measured as either cost per single column inch or cost per thousand readership. While these are valuable guides, they give no indication about coverage by socio-economic groups, geographical area or vocation. This illustration provides for much more detailed information and makes direct comparisons between a number of publications which may be more easily related to the objectives of the company concerned. The illustration is intended to indicate the sort of information the advertiser can use to justify his selection in each publication.

G

Figure 6.6   Press advertising monitor

If the function of advertising is to sell, effectiveness of advertising is to be related where possible to the achievement of its function. The monitor shown in this illustration provides for analysis of inquiries received by publication with an indication of the status of the inquirer. Its particular significance is to indicate to a company the decision maker in any particular inquiring company. Set against these inquiries are ratios for measuring the cost and effectiveness of queries produced. Some publications produce high inquiry responses but may be poor in conversion into orders, thus cost per order would be correspondingly high. This is the only true measure of cost-effectiveness for advertising purposes and is the best method of assessing the extent to which advertising improves sales performance.

FIGURE 6.3

PROGRESS PRODUCTION RECORD

DATE: PREPARED BY:

Publication	Product	Ad. Ref.	Insertion Date	Copy Date	Press Date	Proofs Required	Voucher checked	Account Agreed

FIGURE 6.4

DATE:

SPACE RECORDS

PREPARED BY:

RECORD CARD

Publication		ABC
Address		Circulation
		Readership
Telephone	
Contact	

SIC	Readership		Circulation
1.			
2.			
3.			
4.			
5.			
6.			
7.			
8.			
9.			
10.			
11.			
12.			
13.			
14.			
15.			
16.			
17.			
18.			
19.			
20.			
21.			
22.			
23.			
24.			
25.			
26.			

Copy ......Weeks'   Colour .... Weeks
Classified .... Weeks   Publication ....
Cancellation .... Weeks
Date of latest rate card ....

Standard Rates   Page   Colour   Cover   Special
                  ½ page
                  ¼ page
                  S.C.I.

Mechanical Data
Type page size   Bleed plates
Half page   Column Length
¼ page   Column Width
Trim size   No. of columns
Portrait/Landscape   Screen

A		Region 1	
B		Region 2	
C1		Region 3	
C2		Region 4	
D		Region 5	
E		Region 6	

FIGURE 6.5

SPACE REGISTER

DATE:

PREPARED BY

					PUBLICATION											
CIRCULATION																
READERSHIP																
COST PER SINGLE COLUMN INCH																
COST PER PAGE																
COST PER 1000 CIRCULATION																
COST PER 1000 READERSHIP																
EXPENDITURE PRIOR YEAR ACTUAL																
BUDGETED EXPENDITURE																

FIGURE 6.6

DATE:

PRESS ADVERTISING MONITOR

PREPARED BY:

PUBLICATION	ACTUAL ENQUIRIES						Actual Expenditure	Enquiries Period Circulation	Cost Per Thousand	Orders Booked per thousand	Cost per order
	Board Director	General Manager	Dept. Manager	Senior Executive	Other	Total					

Organisation of Personnel

In the modern business environment the major asset to a company is the calibre of its management and staff. To establish and maintain a lead in the battle for increasing prosperity any successful company develops a sound recruitment policy. Although this is true of all departments, it is particularly true of the marketing department for it provides the major source of contact between the company and its customers. A sound recruitment policy must be continuous, practical and, at times, experimental. By adopting such a policy the company will always be looking for recruits and will encourage colleagues and employees to report on promising material. Although employment may not be immediately available, a suitable candidate should be interviewed and told that he will be advised as soon as a suitable vacancy arises. It is advisable to contact the prospective employee from time to time to reassure him that he has not been forgotten.

To ensure that the recruitment policy remains economic it is not necessary to select automatically the national media for recruitment. If a continuous recruitment policy is maintained there will be a steady stream of applicants which can be vetted as necessary. After a period of time a company will be able to devise the most economic method to attract suitable applicants to ensure an appropriate selection. Each method and each medium should be kept under constant surveillance and measurement of responses, both in quantity and quality, should be recorded. A practical recruitment policy is an integral part of the total marketing plan and the required type of employee can be documented well in advance even to the full period of the marketing plan. It is only by building these short-, medium- and long-term recruitments into the overall marketing plan that a company will be able to recruit in a practical and realistic manner.

In recruiting salesmen, allowances must be made for a certain type of salesman who may eventually become a supervisor. It now seems apparent that good supervisors are not necessarily brilliant salesmen. They are usually good salesmen but will not always appear at the top of the sales performance league. Often the top salesman is a careerist who will go his own brilliant way, rejecting responsibility for control systems and the like, but still bringing in an incredible amount of business. These are not the characteristics of supervisors and such men do not always make good supervisors. In the recruitment programme it is important to ensure that as many top salesmen as possible are recruited and that qualities are sought which eventually lead to a supervisory post.

To satisfy all future needs the company should be seeking different types of people who, initially, will be doing the same kind of job. Many companies have established routines when recruiting. This practice is restrictive and many good people will be missed unless the executive responsible for the recruitment uses his imagination and experiments with different types and methods of recruitment. Providing the type of person the company requires actually exists, it is only a question of contacting them. This, basically, is the recruitment problem. The company should try every method and different media in an effort to obtain the best results. Any advertisement for staff should include details of the type of job being offered, the type of person to fill the job, salary and future prospects. The company recruitment policy is intended to provide a wide enough field to ensure suitable applicants; the purpose of screening is to select those suitable applicants and to narrow the field to the point where the manager will be able to distinguish each applicant in his own mind by his record, prior to the interview. Interviews should be designed initially to provide a shortlist of three or four candidates, not more. From these it should be possible to select one who shows the greatest possibility of early compatibility.

The screening standards are a list of the minimum requirements for the job. The applicant who falls below these standards in any way whatsoever should be rejected. The list should not include things which the company might allow if a candidate meets standards in all other respects. When advertising, it will be necessary to maintain a balance between the need to attract applicants and the screening standards, not only because of the cost but because of the need to preserve confidential information. Sometimes it may be necessary to exclude certain screening standards from the advertisement, but these must be applied when the applications are received. Using screening standards helps to save time by reducing the time senior managers need to reserve for interviewing. It also aids in establishing standards for the job itself.

In practice, marketing is part art and part science. Skill in marketing comes from knowledge and practice of that knowledge. By adopting a realistic training programme a company will give its staff opportunities that will develop the skills necessary to achieve company objectives. Training is now considered a necessity at all levels, and any person in the organisation in contact with customers and prospective customers needs to learn how to deal with those people upon which the future prosperity of the firm will depend. This includes telephone operators, correspondence clerks, receptionists, messengers, delivery drivers, advertising copywriters, public relations staff, typists, accounts clerks and, in particular, installation and maintenance mechanics and salesmen. Salesmen are most frequently in contact with customers; in the minds of most customers the salesman is, in fact, the company.

FIGURE 7.1

JOB SPECIFICATION – MARKETING MANAGER

AUTHORITIES	RESPONSIBILITIES
1. He has authority to recommend the appointment or dismissal of managers reporting to him.	1. All business activities of staff
2. He has authority to approve or disapprove the appointment or dismissal of salesmen and marketing staff.	2. Communications
3. He has authority to recommend plans for sales campaigns.	3. Management and staff merit rating
4. He has authority to recommend the introduction of new products.	4. All sales value and volume
5. He has authority to recommend the policy to be adopted for replacement and make of company cars.	5. Sales performance decisions
6. He has authority to call on technical staff for assistance.	6. Training
7. He has authority to authorise the expenses of his departmental heads and staff.	7. Supervision
8. He has authority to send departmental heads and staff on training courses where warranted.	8. Marketing budget expenditure
9. He has authority to recommend the shows at which the Company should exhibit.	9. Publicity and promotional campaigns
10. He has authority to develop publicity plans and recommendations.	10. Marketing control reports
11. He has authority to recommend appropriate sales forecasts.	11. Equipment used by marketing personnel
12. He has authority to recommend the commissioning of marketing research activities.	12. Sales Literature
13. He has authority for incuring reasonable expenditure for his own travel, hotel and entertaining whilst on company business.	13. Displays and Exhibitions
14. He has authority to use the car provided for him as he thinks fit including his own personal use.	14. Customer complaints
15. He has authority to use time as he thinks best subject to direction by the managing director.	15. Long term planning

FIGURE 7.2			
DATE:		MAN PROFILE	PREPARED BY:

CHARACTERISTICS	Yes	No	INTERVIEWERS NOTES
Physical Make-Up			
1. Appearance			
2. Dress			
3. Health			
Attainments			
4. Education			
5. Technical qualifications			
6. Experience in own industry			
7. Experience			
8. Knowledge of marketing Techn			
9. Ease of manner			
Motivation			
10. Initiative			
11. Ambition			
12. Interest in peace & team work			
.13. Administration & delegation			
14. Job/home relationship			
Intelligence			
15. Analytical ability			
16. Judgement			
17. Evaluation of new ideas			
18. Leadership			
19. Energy Level			
20. Emotional maturity			
21. Loyalty			
22. Decisiveness			
23. Hours of work			
Circumstances			
24. Financial stability			

Historically, sales teams, on the whole, have been recruited in the traditional image of the firm's representatives. Many customers seem, on the surface, to prefer this type of individual because usually he has technical prominence and interest in his product and its uses and gains considerable job satisfaction in developing confidence and amicability with his contacts. Many of these salesmen have only a relatively low degree of selling skill and little appreciation of the need to improve sales performance and reject the need for the application of selling processes. A training course for salesmen should be continuous, otherwise, like a shot of vitamin C, it disappears in the system and is lost. After the main introductory course, training should be provided by the field sales manager, whose coaching and day-to-day leadership control is necessary if selling theories are to be translated into practice on the job.

The salesman of today must fulfil two essential communication functions. He must find customers and potential customers and also provide basic information to his own company for management use.

Figure 7.1   Job specification, marketing manager
Unless each employee knows the exact extent of his responsibilities and the scope of his authority, he will be unable to act with confidence. In the absence of a specification for his job he will not be able to assess his own progress nor develop knowledge or skills relevant to his activities.

The writing of job specifications, particularly for management functions, is a task to be undertaken directly by the company's senior executive and, once introduced, periodically reviewed and amended where necessary, if the company wants to avoid the tendency for individuals to isolate themselves from other executives and to operate independently within the confines of their job specification. As the management team operates in unity, it is the responsibility of the senior executive to direct the day-to-day interpretation of each manager's responsibilities and authorities.

Figure 7.2   Man profile
Job specifications and related man profiles define the job and the man most likely to succeed on the job, thus enabling selection, recruitment, supervision, delegation, training and promotional policies to be effective.

Figure 7.3   Field and sales performance controls

In measuring the performance of each salesman it is normal to compare his actual sales results with a quota set for his territory. The quota for each salesman's territory may be allocated according to product group, by value or by market segment by value. In many companies individual salesman's quotas are allocated according to historical performance. Although this is frequently the simplest means of deciding on quotas, it makes no allowance for variations in territories which can differ by industrial concentration or market segmentation, availability and effectiveness of local advertising media, regional strength of competitors, whether or not it is a development region, or on the company's past record.

So, although the actual performance of salesmen must be recorded and evaluated, it is by itself only a partial measurement.

Figure 7.4   Field sales activity controls

By introducing activity controls it is possible to measure men by market sales potential rather than by actual historical sales turnover. In addition, it is possible to measure the effort and expense that will be required to decide upon local expansion plans, revised delivery facilities, local marketing strategy. Such policy decisions will thus be based on likely profit return rather than through the powers of persuasion of local salesmen or their managers.

Sales revenue achieved in each territory depends upon potential and opportunities open to the man on the spot. While potential can be measured within tolerable limits, opportunity is subject to rapid change. Frequently, due to factors outside the company's immediate control, performance can fluctuate without warning and remedial action is delayed. Effective monitoring can be achieved by analysing, at regular intervals in each territory, the effort devoted by each salesman to achieving his sales turnover. The efforts to be measured are the activities of the salesman and not necessarily the value of the orders he manages to obtain.

Figure 7.5   Merit rating form (salesmen)

In measuring the total effectiveness of the sales force it is necessary to build up an assessment of each individual member. Although the sales performance of the company may be on target, it is

FIGURE 7.3

FIELD SALES PERFORMANCE CONTROLS

DATE:

PREPARED BY:

SALESMAN	Product Group A			Product Group B			Product Group C			Product Group D			Total Product Grps		
	Budget	Actual	Variance	Budget	Actual	Variance	Budget	Actual	Variance	Budget	Actual	Variance	Budget	Actual	Variance

FIGURE 7.4

FIELD SALES ACTIVITY CONTROLS

DATE: PREPARED BY:

TERRITORIAL VARIATIONS	WEIGHTING	SALESMEN ACTIVITIES
1. Size		1. Growth compared with national average
2. Industrial concentration		2. Selling costs/enquiries
3. Market segments		3. Selling Costs/orders
4. Road facilities		4. Selling costs/sales
5. Delivery Service		5. Sales costs to marketing costs
6. Local branch support		6. Number of calls made
7. Local advertising media		7. Number of interviews obtained
8. Strength of competitors		8. Number of enquiries received
9. Development region		9. Number of quotations submitted
10. Company's past reputation		10. Number of orders obtained
11. Political influences		11. Cost per call
12. Decentralised buying		12. Cost per interview
13. Reciprocal trading		13. Average value of orders
14. Strength of local economy		14. Number of orders per clock mileage
15. Pricing policies		15. Average gross margin per order
16.		16. Local advertising against competitors
17.		17. Number of canvasing calls made
18.		18. Average mileage per journey cycle
19.		19. Number of accounts to service
20.		20. Average value of accounts
21.		21. Ratio of customers to prospects
22 .		22 . Number of new accounts opened
23.		23. Number of accounts lost
24.		24.
25.		25.
26.		26.
27.		27.

likely that some salesmen will be exceeding their targets and others are lagging behind. While it is accepted that this situation is typical, it will, nevertheless, not meet the standards necessary in the future. Many such sales forces lack the purpose, enthusiasm and method which can only be provided by lengthy periods of resolute and skilled leadership. One of the basic tasks of such field leadership is to prepare job specifications and related man profiles for a sales function, to define sales territories based on sales potential, to introduce planned selling and, more specifically, selective selling. Field sales managers also act as a communicating force between company and salesmen, and salesmen and company, particularly in establishing the need for targets, quotas and budgets. Above all, a measure of organisational stability must be established in the individual sales task so that the salesman, when taught the techniques of planned selling, will see the advantages to him, as an individual, and will then co-operate in providing self-motivation.

The merit-rating form illustrated is the evaluation by the field sales manager of each salesman for whom he is responsible. When he completes his form he should discuss it in detail with the salesman concerned, giving reasons why he has made the judgement he has recorded and the means by which weaknesses can be overcome and strengths exploited.

Every salesman faces a time problem. Under normal circumstances the only time he can increase sales is when he is, in fact, face to face with the customer. True, in certain circumstances the telephone calls he makes and the letters he writes result in orders. But normally he would sell personally to a customer. In increasing the face-to-face time with buyers it is necessary to reduce the amount of time spent on other activities. By using his time and control sheet each salesman should be able to vet his performance day by day and to decide where time is not being used to best advantage (*Figure 7a*). He will then be able to work out ways in which actual time spent with customers can be increased and non-productive time minimised.

Few companies make the necessary effort to improve the productivity of salesmen by journey planning. Such planning involves the development of low- and high-frequency calls, establishing priorities in terms of customer value and customer potential value, so minimising travelling time, evolving a call pattern, assessing the work load, combining programming flexibility. As salesmen will have accounts of varying sizes, large accounts justify more time than smaller accounts. It is important that management recognises the cost per minute of selling time incurred by salesmen. Often salesmen will spend much time with potential customers who could be substantial buyers. Usually such customers not only buy big but also buy well, but the profitability of such orders, when obtained, does not always justify the effort in winning the order. Often the medium-sized potential customer buying at list price is getting indifferent service from competitors, and is more willing to listen to a proposition.

Figure 7.6   Organisation chart – line functions
In any organisation there will always be some confusion among the staff about who is responsible for certain activities. This is particularly true of telephone operators and receptionists. Frequently members of the sales force are unaware, because of their isolation, of the individuals who hold actual responsibilities for different aspects of company activities. By publishing an organisation chart a company ensures that the significant responsibilities for each of its senior executives are known to all staff. This eases the means of communication and reduces much time and effort expended by employees and, in particular, by customers who may wish to obtain further information or wish to discuss a particular problem with the company.

FIGURE 7.5

MERIT RATING FORM (SALESMEN)

DATE: PREPARED BY:

PERFORMANCE	SPECIFICATION				REMARKS
	Above	Par	Under	Well Under	
Customer Relations					
General					
Prospects					
Complaints					
Objections					
Selling Skill					
Approach					
Presentation					
Closing the Sale					
Product Demonstration					
Technical & Product knowledge					
General					
Industry					
Product					
Pricing					
Awareness					
Benefits					
Personal Organisation					
Reporting & Paperwork					
Maintenance of Records					
Catalogues, Brochures					
Planning of Time					
Customer Records					
Journey Planning					
Personal					
Appearance					
Manner					
Health					

	Week 1	Week 2	Week 3	Week 4	Week 5	Week 6
Figure 7a			TIME PLANNING ANALYSIS SHEET			
Travelling						
Meals						
Entertaining						
Waiting Time						
Preparing Dem.						
Preparing Sales Aids						
Paper Work						
Total Non-Selling Time						
Total Selling Time						
Total Time						

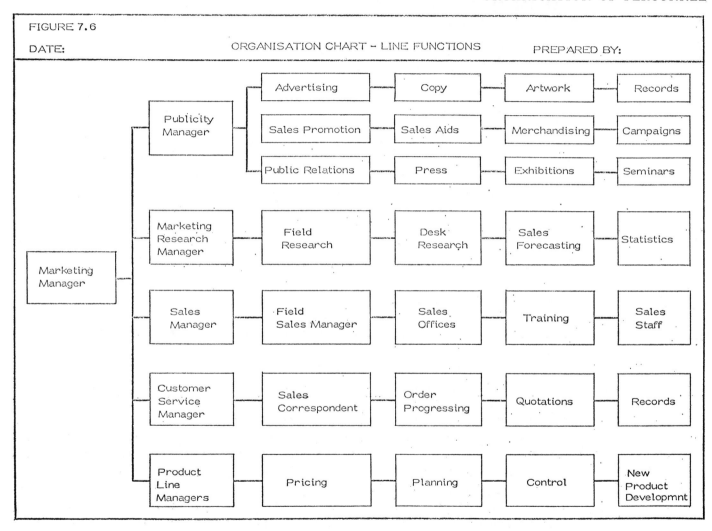

FIGURE 7.6

DATE:

ORGANISATION CHART – LINE FUNCTIONS

PREPARED BY:

8 Arrangement of Budgets

Budgetary control, properly developed, planned and implemented, portrays the entire business operation in a common unequivocable language. Company resources are allocated in predetermined amounts to specific business activities. The expected return is predicted for each of these activities, to provide the maximum possible profit for the enterprise.

Because all forecasts are based on considered judgement the system enables executives to assess the likely alternative courses of action and spotlight the best opportunities. As all alternatives have been considered in advance, any change in operating conditions requiring remedial action becomes a matter of logical decision rather than pure hunch. Deviations from budget can be investigated and the cause isolated. At the time the budgets were set, certain environmental conditions must have been anticipated; investigations into actual conditions should highlight the cause of deviations.

Though the actual implementation of a budgetary control system is essentially an accounting function, it is necessary for the marketing executive to understand fully its workings, functions and practical value. Not only will he be preparing the information fed in but also he will be responsible for its control and for reporting and recommending alternative courses of action should they become necessary.

Because of the complexity of present-day responsibilities of the marketing executive it is essential that the senior marketing executive in a company should be a specialist in general marketing operation. In this way he becomes a businessman in the widest sense of the word with a full understanding and appreciation of the financial control of the marketing function.

As a senior executive, the marketing manager must be completely profit-orientated and, in order to implement profit-making plans, he must understand the nature and the implications of financial accounting. As he is normally responsible for pricing, he will need to be conversant with cost accounting principles and the allocation of company resources towards achieving the required profit on sales irrespective of sales volume or sales growth.

In developing company marketing strategy it is necessary to recognise that the first charge to the business – that is, the first essential cost – is the profit that must be achieved in order to repay shareholders for their investment in the company and for the confidence they have placed in its

FIGURE 8.1

DATE:

MARKETING BUDGET

PREPARED BY:

Prior Yr Actual		Activity	J	F	M	A	M	J	JY	A	S	O	N	D	Full Year	
£	%		£	£	£	£	£	£	£	£	£	£	£	£	£	%
		Budgeted Sales														
		Total Expense														
		Ratios														
///	///	Salaries & Wages														
		Mngt. & Supervision	///	///	///	///	///	///	///	///	///	///	///	///	///	///
		Admin.														
		Salesmen														
		Clerical														
		Other														
		Total														
		Total Headcount														
		Average Remuneration														
///	///	Other expense	///	///	///	///	///	///	///	///	///	///	///	///	///	///
		Asst. Labour Benefits														
		Rent & Rates														
		Communications														
		Travel & Entertaining														
		External Commissions														
		Media Advertising														
		Sales & Literature														
		Public Relations														
		Exhibitions														
		Samples														
		Sales force comm.														
		Misc. Expense														
		Total Other														
		Grand Total														
		Expenses per head														

executives. In preparing his detailed marketing budgets the executive is stating the financial resources the company will need to achieve the sales volume necessary to produce the profit being charged to the business. The marketing function is thus being prepared according to financial investment principles and should be subjected to the monitoring and measuring of performance according to standards adopted for all other forms of investment. The marketing function is not a separate activity capable of measurement in isolation, but is a part of the total company operation within which it must be fully co-ordinated and measured within total performance of the company.

The essence of budgeting is as a control system. By setting budgets the company is establishing high standards, against which actual performance can be measured. Where deviations come to light, explanations can be sought and contingency plans brought into operation to ensure that the profit level is maintained. Until recently financial performance of the company could not be measured – extracting, tabulating and presenting the information was a long-drawn-out process. The information obtained in this way referred to long-passed accounting periods. The causes and counter-measures necessary came too late to be effective.

Today large firms use computers to give them almost instantaneous management information, while small to medium-sized businesses make use of computer bureaux or, even more effectively, computer terminals. The use of electronic data processing equipment makes it easier to employ management information systems and to prepare budgets for control purposes. In future years more companies will make use of computer power to program alternative sets of operating conditions to assess the effects of marketing strategy and marketing tactics on the company's profitability. Effectively, this is a form of trial and error using simulation instead of actual business environment. This minimises the consequences of inappropriate decisions to nothing more than the expenditure on stationery used by the computer's printing equipment.

The actual deployment of resources adopted by the marketing executive to achieve the objectives of the business is commonly known among marketing men as the marketing mix. It is the total blend of resources expressed in purely financial terms, incorporating the elements, manpower, time and energy devoted to exploiting a current and anticipated market situation. It is on the assessment and realisation of prevailing conditions that marketing prosperity depends. By choosing the most vulnerable area for penetration, and devoting the company's resources to that point, the market-orientated company ensures its own prosperity.

It is in the use of budgeting operations that the term management by objectives has come into

FIGURE 8.2																
				ANALYSIS OF MARKETING EXPENSE										PREPARED BY:		
DATE:																
Prior Yr Two		Prior Year			Current Year		Plan Yr One		Plan Yr Two		Plan Yr Three		Plan Yr Four		Plan Yr Five	
£	+- %	£	+- %	Activity	£	+- %	£	+- %	£	+- %	£	+- %	£	+- %	£	+- %
				Labour												
				Salaries												
				Entertaining												
				Travelling												
				Car expenses												
				Subscriptions												
				Recruitment												
				Training												
				Telephone & Telex												
				Stationery												
				Postage												
				Office Equipment												
				Professional Fees												
				Rent												
				Rates												
				Insurance												
				Lighting												
				Heating												
				Repairs												
				Commercial Vehicles												
				Hire												
				Catering												
				Depreciation												
				Warehousing												
				Carriage												
				Public Relations												
				Press Advertising												
				Sales Promotion												
				Total												

common usage. The use of management information systems in the modern business environment has resulted in the creation of a volume of paperwork which would prove a fulltime job for the ordinary executive to process. Using properly controlled budget systems, responsible executives should receive only information on activities which show a significant deviation from budget and for which corrective action is required. Where actual results prove better than those budgeted, the executive concerned will be advised also of the situation so that a favourable situation can be further exploited.

The financial liquidity of any company is dependent on an adequate flow of revenue to cover all out-goings. Frequently, new product launches or the recruitment of additional staff requires an initial investment which can only be recovered at some time in the distant future. In order to retain a positive cash flow situation the financial controller will need to have advance warning of such investments in order to obtain the necessary funds. When the entire business operation is properly planned and all activities are subjected to budgetary control, the financial controller should be able to utilise fully the company's assets so as to avoid unnecessary borrowing at high interest rates to finance investments.

Figure 8.1   Marketing budget
This illustration shows in outline the standard categories of expense for marketing activities – the marketing mix. It shows expenditure for each month of the budgeted year and provides useful control ratios, as a guide to marketing productivity.

The total marketing expense is related to budgeted sales both for the prior and actual periods and for the full year ahead. The percentage indicator against each pound spent is used to indicate the interrelationship between individual items. There is provision for showing the average remuneration of management and staff for each month of the year. It also shows the marketing expense per employee as an indication of pressures on recruitment.

Figure 8.2   Analysis of marketing expense
This form shows marketing expense within the full period of the marketing plan and isolates in detail the various expenses incurred in the administration and implementation of marketing policies.

FIGURE 8.3

DATE:

ALLOCATION OF EXPENSE

PREPARED BY:

Activity	performance last year 19 .... = 100	Total Assets Last Year	Return on Assets last year	Variance – last year budget +– %	Total Assets Forecast	Return on Assets forecast	TOTAL BUDGET SOUGHT			% + – last year	Management Rating	Priority weighting total = 100%	Allocation approved
							Amount	Minimum % performance	Maximum % performance				

FIGURE 8.4

DATE:

COST CENTRES

PREP ARED BY:

Headcount			Cost Centre	Expense						
Budget	Actual	Variance		Current Month Budget	Current Month Actual	Current Month Variance	Comulat- ive Budget	Comulat- ive Actual	Comulat- ive Variance	Red Flag Action
			Marketing Research							
			Publicity							
			Planning							
			Administration							
			Distribution							
			Sales Force							
			Totals							

Actual expenditure for each year during the course of the plan is plotted and the percentage increase or decrease year by year is featured.

Figure 8.3　Allocation of expense

It is a principle of budgeting that the person responsible for controlling a budget should also be responsible for working out the expenditure he will need to incur to achieve the tasks he has been allocated. In giving him this responsibility the company's management will expect him to carry out a detailed investigation into the resources he will require and to provide justification for his recommendations.

In operating successfully, every company needs to make maximum use of the limited resources it is able to make available. Allowing executives to develop their own budgets ensures that the responsible manager has every confidence in his staff achieving the performance required. However, the most responsible of executives tend to overestimate as they allow psychologically for the unexpected. There is, almost every time, room for some pruning, although these cuts should be made in the presence, and with the general approval, of the executive responsible.

Senior management is responsible for co-ordinating the activities of its executives. To allow each ambitious manager to develop his plans in complete isolation from other departments is fundamentally wrong to business planning principles. Each manager must be given an adequate briefing on the tasks expected of him in the period under review and he must submit budgets to achieve these tasks. When all budgets have been submitted, all activities should be co-ordinated by senior management and available funds allocated accordingly. Some activities will require greater priority than others and the spread of funds will be determined according to priorities.

In this illustration provision has been made for the manager's own assessment of the maximum and minimum performance which he would expect to achieve if his full budget were approved.

Figure 8.4　Cost centres

In making individual managers fully responsible for the control of their own department operations, it is necessary for budgets to be prepared for each department, and for actual performance against budget to be reported against each budget period.

In departmentalising budgets the company is creating cost centres which, though an integral

Prior Yr Actual	Product Group	J	F	M	A	M	J	JY	A	S	O	N	D	Full Year
	Budget													
	Actual													
	% achievement													
	% performance													
	Budget													
	Actual													
	% achievement													
	% performance													
	Budget													
	Actual													
	% achievement													
	% performance													
	Budget													
	Actual													
	% achievement													
	% performance													
	Budget													
	Actual													
	% achievement													
	% performance													
	Budget													
	Actual													
	% achievement													
	% performance													
Total	Budget													
	Actual													
	% achievement													
	% performance													

FIGURE 8.5

BUDGETS CONTROL

DATE:

PREPARED BY:

part of the total company operation, have been given almost autonomous control, but subject to policy and financial dictation laid down by the company. Not all of these cost centres will be revenue raising, but their performances will be measured against the specific objectives set for their achievement at the time the plan was produced.

The cost centres shown on this illustration are for the normal marketing activity groupings typical of many businesses. Companies may develop their own categories and, hence, cost centres, according to the requirements of their own operations. Apart from the head count that is recorded on the form, there is provision for month-by-month expenditure and for cumulative expenditure with variances against each period. In the final column the red flag action feature should be provided and, where necessary, an indication of remedial action can be itemised.

Figure 8.5   *Budget control*

Many companies prefer to budget their expenditure according to product groups, particularly where they have introduced the product group manager as part of the implementation of marketing principles. The product group manager, under these circumstances, is usually responsible for the profitability of the products within his group, and will draw on the services of the sales force and marketing services department in order to promote his products and achieve his profit forecast.

Some companies may use the same basic format shown but delegate profit responsibility to an area or branch manager who has responsibility for a given geographical area and whose performance is measured by achievement against budget according to a given percentage for his area. Other companies allocate this responsibility to marketing managers who have a similar function to product group managers but provide a full range of the company's products to specific market segments.

Figure 8.6   *Decision budgets*

A company may delay making a decision involving the contraction of a particular activity in the hope that it will right itself after a given period of time. Frequently this means that the financial consequences resulting from that activity are much more pronounced because of a delayed decision. Once the deterioration has become apparent, every effort should be made to rectify the situation. If, at the time of planning, a contingency programme has been drawn up, at a given point of decline

FIGURE 8.6

DECISION BUDGETS

DATE: PREPARED BY:

Activity	J	F	M	First quarter review	A	M	J	Second quarter review	JY	A	S	Third quarter review	O	N	D
Annual budget															
Annual actual															
Annual variance															
decreasing conting ency															
Annual budget															
Annual actual															
Annual variance															
decreasing conting ency															
Annual budget															
Annual actual															
Annual variance															
decreasing conting ency															
Annual budget															
Annual actual															
Annual variance															
decreasing conting ency															
Annual budget															
Annual actual															
Annual variance															
decreasing conting ency															
Annual budget															
Annual actual															
Annual variance															
decreasing conting ency															
Total Annual budget															
Annual actual															
Annual variance															
decreasing conting ency															

126

the activity will either be jettisoned or completely restructured. The subsequent developments are then more likely to be soundly conceived. Decisions may be made under considerable stress and are difficult to make rationally. The best time to make a decision affecting the jobs of colleagues or the activities of a department or of a product is when, in possession of all the facts, it can be arrived at calmly and without emotion.

9 Provision of Contingencies

A company is like a living being—it has a brain, a heart, a personality and a reputation, and, like any living organism, must adapt to its environment in order to survive. The appetite of a company is nourished by profit and the greater the nourishment, greater grows the appetite. In modern business philosophy there is only one rational reason for any business activity and that is the maximisation of profits. Many social service and patriotic policies for which some companies are well known are but secondary objectives and are frequently adopted to provide a favourable public image.

No matter how carefully a business may plan, certain objectives will always prove more difficult to achieve than others. Marketing planning is no panacea for all industrial and commercial ills. Ideally, the marketing plan should include the appropriate action to be taken in order to avoid diminution of profitability. Even if actual performance exceeds all expectations, there should be provision for further exploitation of the favourable conditions that have been discovered. If the total marketing plan has been constructed with care and diligence, the contingency section should be straightforward, being no more than the detailed consideration of alternative courses of action. The contingency plan should include action that may need to be adopted in the short term to minimise or maximise possible consequences of deviations from plan, and medium- to long-term action to exploit a changed environment.

To ensure that the appropriate action is taken at a time calculated to produce best results, it is essential that a barometer of company and industrial performance is developed and steps are taken to monitor actual results against forecast company sales and forecast market shares. There are some specialist organisations providing performance comparisons within an industry at reasonable cost. A company using such an organisation will need to develop only an internal early warning system. This can be done effectively for the long term by plotting orders received by major product groups against the purchasing industry by standard industrial classification.

In the short term, signals can be provided by relating actual inquiries, quotations, orders received and sales by major groups, against the forecast objectives. If the average time-lag between inquiry and order is six weeks and a delivery period four to six weeks, then, automatically, the company will have nearly three months' notice of an imminent drop in sales. For example, if the company volume in value of inquiries is only 80 per cent of the forecast, and the conversion ratio remains unchanged, in three months' time sales will only be 80 per cent of target. While it would be unwise to take remedial action against one deviation from forecast (for fluctuations do occur), once a trend becomes apparent on the graph the cause will be established and appropriate action can be taken.

Apart from showing industrial performance as a whole, some specialist organisations quote the detailed performance of unspecified companies against which one's own company performance can be measured. At this point the company should be able to judge to what extent it will be able to exercise influence on the market situation. If the entire industry is suffering a similar deteriorating position, it is probably wise to curtail expansion plans, as provided within the contingency plan. The timing of such cutbacks, and to what extent they are implemented, should be incorporated into the total marketing plan. The plan should show detailed profit and loss statements for 70 per cent, 80 per cent, 90 per cent, 110 per cent and 120 per cent actual performance against forecast. Each of the profit and loss accounts should include appropriate departmental budgets and head counts. The two major driving principles are to preserve a net profit and to indemnify future net profit. Often, in practice, these two considerations prove incompatible and a working compromise may be warranted. Sometimes profit comes from the last 15 to 20 per cent of sales, after overheads have been covered and when costs become marginal. Under such circumstances a drop of 20 per cent in sales volume will warrant perhaps a cut of 30 per cent in expenditure in order to maintain net profit at par value.

Occasionally a company can avoid the disasters of a temporarily poor market position by acquisition of another company. Study of the competitive profiles in the marketing plan, followed by a detailed investigation of suitable partners, may reveal a competitor which would supplement or, ideally, complement the company's own operation. The first consideration will always be to make a take-over bid, but realistic management must not discount the advantage of soliciting for a bid to be made for one's own company—this course of action may prove more prudent.

A logical part of any contingency plan should be a detailed consideration of both rationalisation and diversification policies. There is almost always conflict between a company's sales department, anxious to meet individual customer requirements, and the production department needing long production runs and the elimination of cost-consuming specials. Some firms have reconciled these opposing needs by adopting a market segmentation policy and produce specials for each industry group. They have become so well established within these industries that they have achieved long production runs of specials. While these firms have concentrated their efforts and production on

I

that part of the market for which they are best suited, others have diversified into other activities in order to take up their surplus production capacity.

The essence of rationalisation is the opportunity created to obtain economies of large-scale production. The increasing use of automation has made it possible for high volume production at a lower unit cost. A bigger, faster machine will not, normally, need more work-people to attend to it. Premises will not necessarily be different, therefore economies are possible immediately on the labour content of production and on the overheads of plant per unit of output. Though purchases of raw materials will increase in volume proportionate to production, economies are still possible by obtaining discounts for bulk purchases. For a substantial buyer, improvements in the quality of delivery and service may also be obtained.

Because of the specialisation adopted it should be possible to recruit or train specialists in particular work categories and so ensure a better quality of personnel and performance. Certain administrative economies are also possible. It is unlikely that clerical costs will keep pace with the increase in output. These economies are more likely to be achieved during the early stages of growth, as the current tendency is for administrative costs to rise to a rate consistent with the increasing complexity of management operations.

The elements of marketing will not rise in the same proportion as the increase in output. A full-page advertisement in a newspaper or magazine will cost the same, whatever the volume of business. Market research studies of the same scale will cost no more, whatever the size of firm, and salesmen are recruited normally according to the number of customers and prospects rather than sales turnover or sales potential. In practice, larger firms do spend more on these marketing functions in order to achieve additional benefits. The bigger the advertising appropriation, the easier it is to find an agency with a wide range of skills and services. Advertising may be used more effectively as a result. A broader blanket study should bring more and better facts for decision making, so reducing the risk element and minimising the waste of resources. It could mean that the company would be able to promote, and then exploit, its product's potential more effectively. A larger firm may also be able to provide better training facilities for salesmen and, as a result, produce an improvement in sales performance.

Larger firms nearly always have the advantage over smaller firms when borrowing money. Frequently the rate of interest charged will vary according to the size of organisation. Because larger firms are considered less of a risk, the interest rate may be as much as 1 per cent less than that applied to smaller companies.

FIGURE 9.1

STANDARD COSTS—BY PRODUCT IN PERIOD

DATE: PREPARED BY:

COST ITEM	this period standard costs	last period standard costs	this period actual costs	last period actual costs	this period standard costs per unit	last period standard costs per unit	this period actual costs per unit	last period actual costs per unit	this period standard over actual	last period standard over actual	this period actual over standard	last period actual over standard	this period prior yr actual =100	last period prior yr actual =100
Manufactured material														
Bought-in parts														
Purchased material														
Overhead														
Labour														
Total Manufacturing														
Salaries & Wages														
Overhead														
Total Administration														
Salaries & Wages														
Overhead														
Total Research & Development														
Salaries & Wages														
Advertising														
Public Relations														
Sales Promotion														
Marketing Research														
Consultancy Services														
Product Line														
Distribution														
Direct selling expense														
Total Marketing Costs														
Total Costs														

FIGURE 9.2

PRICING SCHEDULE

DATE:

PREPARED BY:

PRODUCT	Volume A Breakeven Point					Volume B 10% Return						Volume C 20% Return					
	MNFG Costs		O.H. & marketing		Unit Price	MNFG Costs		O.H. & marketing		Unit Price	g.m.	MNFG Costs		O.H. & marketing		Unit Price	g.m.
	Fix-ed	Vari able	Fix-ed	Vari able	shillings	Fix-ed	Vari able	Fix-ed	Vari able	shillings	%	Fix-ed	Vari able	Fix-ed	Vari able	shillings	%

The larger firm may be able to deal with and maintain its own laboratories, recruit its own skilled specialist researchers, and retain full rights to discoveries and developments made by its own research activities. By the provision of subsidised canteen facilities, sports and social clubs, sickness and pension schemes, and wider promotion prospects, a larger firm is able to foster goodwill, loyalty and high morale amongst its employees—all ingredients of efficiency.

A diversification policy may be adopted, in order to spread the risk of activity across a broader front, so minimising business risk. Many of the economies of scale may be achieved with a diversification policy.

It frequently happens that additional marketing costs necessary to fill surplus capacity from the established market, with an established product, are uneconomic because of competitive pressures. The spare capacity available may be used more profitably for another product, possibly in a different market. When products reach saturation point company growth is confined to that obtainable at the expense of competitors. Government economic measures are, frequently, the cause of sudden changes in demand. Companies adversely affected by such a change have no alternative but to diversify if they wish to survive. Many products are traditionally seasonal, and manufacturers of these products must endeavour to stimulate sales at other times of the year or to move into other fields. It is not always possible to pass on increasing costs to the customer by raising selling prices— either because of competitive pressures or because the market will not bear it. Some firms have adopted a strategic diversification by offering a related facility in order to sell its regular product.

Where there is a strong possibility that a scientific break-through will bring product obsolescence, affected companies should endeavour to concentrate future plans upon a less vulnerable field of operations. A side-step into a related industry or technology is a natural and logical move for most companies, for it is an area where their technology and management expertise may be put to best use.

Figure 9.1 Standard costs by a product in period
The profit on any particular product varies according to the number of units manufactured at any one time. In forecasting its future profitability every company must endeavour to establish its basic economic manufacturing batch. The whole basis of sales forecasting is to provide the production department with advance warning of required volume. Inaccurate forecasts mean inevitably a build-up of stock, and this means production schedules have to be varied from day

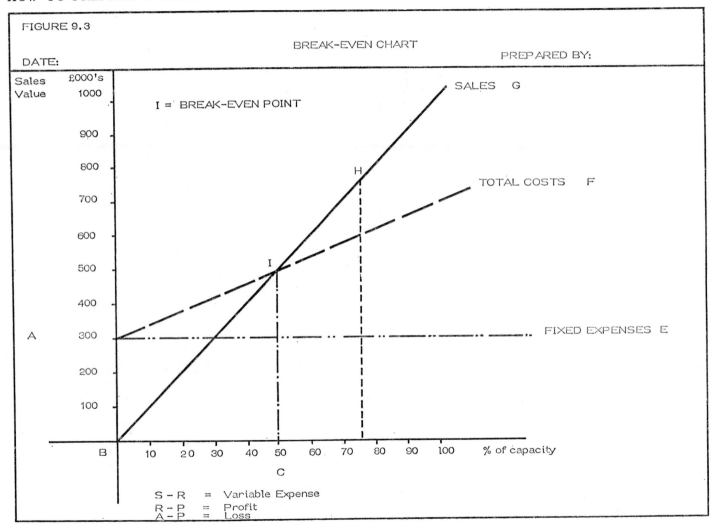

FIGURE 9.3

BREAK-EVEN CHART

DATE:

PREPARED BY:

Sales Value £000's

I = BREAK-EVEN POINT

SALES   G

TOTAL COSTS   F

FIXED EXPENSES E

% of capacity

S – R = Variable Expense
R – P = Profit
A – P = Loss

to day, with uneconomic batches produced. To assess the consequences of these events, each company should prepare a standard cost for each product against which every trading cost makes a contribution. The standard costs are those which are expected to be incurred when the product is being manufactured in its most economic quantity and against which actual costs as incurred during trading can be compared. The cost structure shown in this illustration provides many combinations of costing criteria, each of which can be used as control figures in estimating end-of-year profit based on actual operating costs compared to the standard costs.

Figure 9.2   Pricing schedule

Many companies have built a successful organisation based on the bulk of production being sold at a price which recovers all operating costs and relying on the balance of sales to provide a profit. In certain circumstances this policy can be justified, but it must always be based upon a position of strength rather than one of weakness.

All markets have a broad range of pricing sectors with the majority of suppliers concentrating around the competitive area. The strong firms predominate in the higher price sector and the weaker firms are found usually in the low price sector. There is constant pressure within individual companies to push prices towards the top of the pricing range while its market is endeavouring to deflate the pricing structure. Usually the argument for reducing prices is the increase in volume which it is expected will result; conversely, it is always possible that the same volume will be achieved even if prices are raised. Whether a company decides on a high price or a low price, the ability of its sales force and the power of its promotional activities will need to be superior to those of competitors if the market potential is to be fully exploited. A company will need to provide strong supporting services for buyers to be willing to pay a premium price for its products. Similarly, buyers do not change sources of supply giving them good service over a period of time simply to obtain a marginal price advantage.

Figure 9.3   Break-even chart

Once a company has established standard costs for each item in its range, based upon expected volume for each product, it is able to work out the variable costs which must be incurred during the period of the manufacturing cycle. Ideally, in preparing for all contingencies, the company

	FIGURE 9.4									
				LOST BUSINESS AND OPPORTUNITIES						
DATE:								PREPARED BY:		
Prospect Name	geographical Area	S.I.C.	Product Group	Value at Par	% gross margin	Amount in Budget	Contingency Action Proposed	Value	Target Date	Rating %

should chart a break-even point at all levels of sales achieved and at every percentage point of manufacturing capacity. Once the break-even point has been established for each level, it becomes possible for the company to apply varied selling prices to different industrial groups in order to achieve maximum penetration according to sales potential within each group. Certain industries often have a more fundamental need for particular products than others, and additional marketing costs can be incurred in penetrating a particular industry or industries, especially where there is a high degree of elasticity in demand, based significantly on price. By varying its pricing structure according to industry and according to the demand within each industry, a company is best able to exploit the conflicting demands of sales volume and low price and high margins at low volume.

Figure 9.4   Lost business and opportunities
Senior management of many companies is reluctant to admit that its products are not of a suitable standard, that its pricing strategy is at fault or that its total marketing effort is misdirected or weak. It is only by evaluating carefully the reasons for lost business and opportunities that the weaknesses of a company's operations become apparent. Every significant inquiry not resulting in an order should be recorded, and the reasons why the business was lost investigated. Every effort should be made to develop a method of overcoming that weakness so that future inquiries can be processed with earlier faults rectified.

Of much more significance are the opportunities lost because an inquiry was never given to the company in the first place. It may be because the company has not informed its market adequately of the products it has to offer, nor of the services that it provides. It may be because the sales force is not concentrating enough effort on winning the new business, because it is too busy dealing with established customers and not making enough cold calls, or because the sales force is simply weak in presenting the company to its prospects.

Frequently, causes can be isolated if the company splits business and opportunities into geographical areas, standard industrial classifications or product groups. Weaknesses can then be isolated according to their significance to the company and its markets.

Figure 9.5   Rationalisation schedule
It is not unusual for a company that has been in existence for several years to carry in its range

FIGURE 9.5												
				RATIONALISATION SCHEDULE								
DATE:										PREPARED BY:		
PRODUCT	Unit Direct Costs	Unit Indirect Costs	% manufactg capacity	% total sales	% sales force costs	% publicity costs	% total marketg costs	average delivery period	sales trend last ten years yr 1 =100	sales trend last 12 mths mth 1=100	expected product sales life mths	expected product withdrawal date

FIGURE 9.6

DATE:

CONTINGENCY ACTION PLAN

	Budget Figure to date	Actual Figure to date	Variance Figure to date	% performance against budget	Budget Figure Year end	Forecast Figure Year end	Variance Figure Year end	% performance Year end	Action Yr End forecast 80%	90%	110%	120%
Sales product Grp A												
Grp B												
Grp C												
Grp D												
Total Sales												
Gross Margin												
Marketing Expenses												
1. salaries & wages												
2. vehicles												
3. publicity												
4. rent and rates												
5. commissions												
6. depreciation												
7. govt. charges												
8. taxes												
9. interest charges												
10. other expenses												
Net profit												
Employees												
1. mngt. & supervsr												
2. salesmen												
3. administration												
4. clerical												
5. other												
Notes on Courses of Action												

products that have long lost significance to the greater proportion of its customers and are being bought only by customers who stick to traditional products and ideas. Obviously, a progressive company does not want to rely for future business and prosperity upon customers not prepared to meet modern conditions. Once a product has lost its usefulness it is far better to remove it from the range completely, rather than to produce uneconomical quantities and carry stocks of slow-moving products which, in all probability, do not even make a realistic profit contribution.

It is only when operating cost analysed into major sections is compared to other products that some indication of its value becomes apparent.

In the form used are sections for viewing trends for a product over a period of ten years with year 1 having an index of 100 and a sales trend pattern for the last twelve months with month 1 having an index of 100. From this information it is possible to assess the future sales life of a product consistent with its profit contribution, and to programme the date at which the product is likely to be withdrawn from the range.

Figure 9.6   Contingency action plan
As profit is the first charge to the business enterprise, but inevitably, in practical terms, it is the money left over at the end of the year's trading, it is imperative that the forecast of performance, from which profit is derived, is forecast as early as possible in each operating year. After some four of five months of the trading year it should be possible to establish trends from which end of year results can be predicted. Obviously, because no company operates in isolated periods, and its trading is continuous, monthly results for the previous year, month by month, can be used as the foundations against which the results in the current year can be accumulated. This provides an established pattern over many months of activity, so allowing a measure for projection into the future, to the end of the current year. Where the trend shows an unsatisfactory result, remedial action may be taken well in advance, providing that variations in operating costs can be isolated and their cause established.

Realisation of Plans 10

Need for improved efficiency and the constant search for improved productivity have long been accepted for manufacturing processes in industry. A similar need has been recognised for some time in the marketing function, but has never been resolved satisfactorily because of the difficulties in developing and applying accounting principles to a business activity which is considered part art and part science. Although many marketing activities operate under disciplines not widely appreciated, let alone understood, by management, the practice of marketing is still an investment in company resources and, if control is to be maintained, will be subject to the same accounting appraisal as any other form of investment. In using the principles and charts set out in this book, it is possible for various costs to be collated and analysed so that the expenditure on marketing activities and their effects upon profitability can be ascertained. Activities are shown by customer and by products, some of which may prove unprofitable on investigation.

If stock levels are controlled with great accuracy the cost of handling orders of various sizes can be ascertained. It may be more profitable to refuse orders below a certain uneconomic level. Such selective selling often increases profitability. The location of warehouses, the planning of sales territories and the routes of salesmen can be planned, based on accurate cost statistics rather than by intuition. Improved direction and supervision of salesmen by the setting of performance and activity targets can increase selling and operating efficiency.

Management of many businesses is unable to recognise that its products or service are mediocre and sometimes inferior. Where such blindness exists the company is unlikely to introduce methods or procedures which would help to rectify or overcome the problem. Under such circumstances the company is unlikely to experiment with new ideas or to make a fresh approach in an effort to improve its future prosperity. Probably the only avenue left open for that firm is to continue in its historical fashion, no matter how much the position may deteriorate.

Technological change is causing a greater demand for information to be employed in decision making. As companies grow, investment decisions become vast and more complex and the businessman must endeavour to forecast growth potential and factors likely to influence his company's penetration of that potential, in an effort to reduce the risk facing every business enterprise. In marketing there has long been a need to concentrate information into quantitative and yet practical forms, to provide the basis for a company's marketing information system and to help ensure more effective marketing control and the development of increased profit opportunity. The effect of marketing planning and the integration of the marketing *function* into proper accounting procedures is intended to produce a higher return than would be possible in totalling the performance of the constituent parts.

Companies should be able to state the influences on their major activities and how they are being controlled to the benefit of the total organisation. They should be able to assess the extent to which the information provided is relevant to current management needs. Executives need to eliminate unused material being prepared and to discover additional information. Such research into the marketing effort will help to ensure that the most economic level of expenditure is being maintained. For marketing, planning and control will help to reduce misdirected effort in all promotional activities by selective selling policies and the concentration of publicity, energy and expense, thus reducing the actual cost of producing and selling goods. Appropriate marketing policies should ensure that all products are developed according to market needs and resources are not wasted on products unsatisfactory in the market place.

The recent change of emphasis to impersonal selling techniques, such as advertising, is one of the more important developments in marketing consumer goods. Personal selling still has an important role in industrial marketing. Improvement in the function and performance of industrial sales forces justifies more attention than is now necessary in the consumer goods selling effort. Unless they are given adequate direction, salesmen cannot be expected to sell the ideal product mix nor can they, without guidance, differentiate between products when considering profitability. The level of profit responsibility must be not only decided but widely communicated, to ensure satisfactory implementation of the most critical of business activities.

The marketing plan and all documents ancillary to the plan must be used by executives as a day-to-day evaluation control and development manual. Every effort should be taken to avoid treating the planning process as a once-a-year political exercise which is suffered by busy executives performing other tasks. Planning, organisation, direction and control are the basic jobs of management; in a successful marketing-orientated company they will fill the working day of the management. Each manager must understand the interactive nature of the individual tasks which have to be completed during each period of the marketing plan. The timing of each step, at all levels and in each function, is critical if the total plan is to be satisfactorily co-ordinated and the anticipated results achieved. A flexible attitude to planning principles must be adopted so that management recognises the need for contingencies and the control of contingencies within corporate strategy. Unforeseen events

FIGURE 10.1

MAJOR ACTION PROGRAMME

DATE: PREPARED BY:

MANAGER	STAND BY	ACTION AND COMPLETION DATE												Following Year			
		J	F	M	A	M	J	JY	A	S	O	N	D	¼	½	¾	1
MARKETING MANAGER									Revise marketing strategy programme								
PUBLICITY MANAGER			Prepare new sales literature														
MARKETING RESEARCH MANAGER						Research market by S.I.C.											
SALES MANAGER											Report new sales office location						
CUSTOMER SERVICE MANAGER		Develop new progressing system															
PRODUCT LINE MANAGER						Produce new product programme											
FIELD SALES MANAGER												Write new sales manual					
BRANCH MANAGER		Recommend new journey cycles															
PERSONNEL MANAGER										Select staff with Management potential							

often create a different scale of priorities; flexibility in the interpretation of policy as provided for in the plan must be recognised if the company's interests are to be best served. The results of monitoring actual performance against forecasts have a definite value in personnel development and in operating efficiency, as does the preparation of forecasts itself.

In every marketing-orientated company final responsibility for marketing policies remain with the chief executive. The marketing manager of any company provides advice in the field of marketing and may well carry a line responsibility, but if the marketing concept is to be adopted the entire company, and in particular the management team, must be devoted towards its customers' satisfaction.

In the immediate future most businesses will become involved increasingly with computerisation. Even if not directly involved as users, companies will become affected by the use to which suppliers, competitors and even customers have become enmeshed with electronic data processing. It is essential that every businessman should see how the computer is applied to marketing problems. He needs some appreciation of the effects of computers on present-day marketing decisions and upon future decisions. At present management has tended to utilise computers for administration and control because they are close to the accounting function. Little use of data processing techniques has been made in decision making because they often involve operational research techniques.

Computers will be used increasingly in the management sections covered in this book. The most critical areas in which marketing decisions are desirable are in the efforts to measure changes in the pattern of demand for a product. As yet no recognisable relationship has been established between marketing action and swings in demand. As more information is gathered by companies using the working methods recommended, more definite patterns will begin to emerge and, eventually, levels of sales will be forecast according to predetermined marketing action. The most notable feature will be the elimination of the traditional walls between departments.

Computers are capable of performing most clerical functions and, when stripped of their clerical duties, little is left of normal office procedures, whether they are in a buying or a sales office. Their functions can be fully integrated as a much smaller unit, while there may be an increase in absolute numbers of top management. The future growth potential of computer-linked terminals, particularly those operating on a real time service basis, making virtually full computerisation possible and economic for most smaller firms, will assist in the rapid trend towards scientific application of marketing.

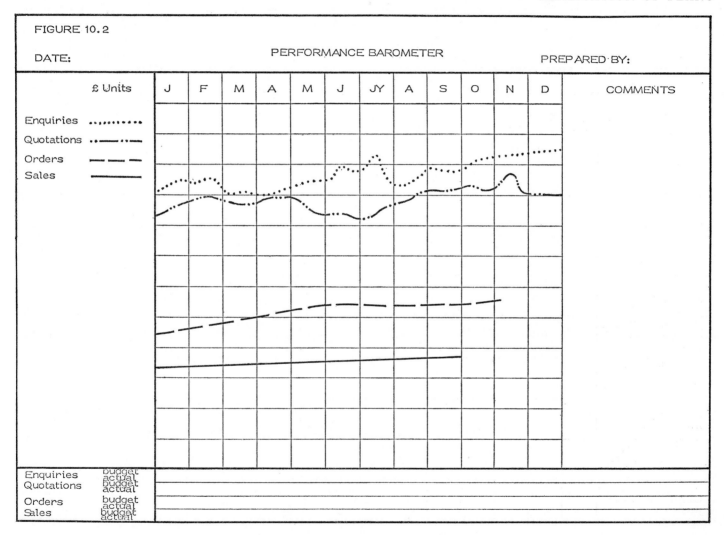

FIGURE 10.2

DATE:

PERFORMANCE BAROMETER

PREPARED·BY:

	£ Units	J	F	M	A	M	J	JY	A	S	O	N	D	COMMENTS
Enquiries													
Quotations													
Orders													
Sales													

Enquiries — budget / actual
Quotations — budget / actual
Orders — budget / actual
Sales — budget / actual

FIGURE 10.3

MANAGEMENT CONTROL RATIOS

DATE: PREPARED BY:

RATIOS	Operating Profit/ Operating Assets	Operating Profit/ Sales %	Sales/Operating Assets (times per yr)	Production costs of Sales	Distribution and Marketing Costs	General and Administration costs	Materials Costs	Works Labour Costs	Other production costs	Operating Assets	Current Assets	Fixed Assets	Stocks	Work in Progress	Debtors	Land, Buildings	Plant, Machinery Equipment, vehicles
RETURN ON ASSETS																	
PROFIT MARGIN ON SALES																	
TURNOVER OF ASSETS																	
DEPARTMENTAL COSTS % OF SALES																	
PRODUCTION COSTS % OF SALES VALUE OF PRODUCTION																	
GENERAL ASSET USAGE £'s PER £1000 OF SALES																	
CURRENT ASSET USAGE £'s PER £1000 OF SALES																	
FIXED ASSET USAGE £'S PER £1000 OF SALES																	

FIGURE 10.4   COMPUTER PRINT OUT

DATE:							PREPARED BY:	

BATCH 01 SHEET 001   AUTONOMICS LTD. 308–316 Euston Road, London NW1
                                                                    3BU

CUSTOMER PERFORMANCE

ACCOUNT NUMBER	ACCOUNT NAME	TURNOVER THIS MONTH	TURNOVER THIS YEAR	TURNOVER LAST YEAR	TURNOVER DIFFERENCE
A04037	M CONTRACTORS	£ 1143	£ 9830	£ 507	95%+
A06007	STAR ELECTRICS	£ 7864	£ 9175	£ 306	97%+
A11420	WELCROSE LTD.	£ 83886	£104857	£ 7224	93%+
A16051	MATTHEW WALL	£ 62914	£ 83986	£ 8192	90%+
B29745	HOWITT CO LTD.	£ 17367	£ 18353	£ 986	94%+
B41557	E & C LTD.	£ 1003	£ 10158	£ 557	95%+
B53359	SUN ELECTRICS	£ 1403	£ 11141	£ 983	91%+
B63541	SANTON CO LTD	£ 162	£ 983	£ 0	109%+
X63894	FLINDERS & CO.	£ 21299	£ 22282	£ 2294	90%+
A75635	PHOENIX CO.	£ 14090	£ 14745	£ 1310	91%+
A77033	P ELECTRICAL,	£ 357	£ 983	£ 327	72%+
A77772	VOGUE LTD.	£ 60	£ 985	£ 150	92%+
A78000	MODERNELECTRIC	£ 39	£ 655	£ 0	100%+
A89829	LM ELECTRICAL	£ 0	£ 0	£ 0	0%
A90011	TWNAM CO.	£ 0	£ 0	£ 0	0%

K *

Figure 10.1   Major action programme

In a properly co-ordinated management policy programme each planned activity must have direct and indirect consequences on all other planned activities. Eventually all management actions are interrelated and it is imperative that every task assigned to individual managers should have a clearly specified time of action and established completion date. Even senior managers need the discipline of an agreed deadline date for the finalisation of reports and project activities. By including major management actions in the marketing plan, other managers become aware of the activities of their colleagues and will be able to see the effects of each other's activities on all other functions as a clear policy of objectives is established and co-ordinated. Ideally, a standby should be nominated for each task, reducing to a minimum any delay caused by the nominated executive becoming ill or being otherwise indisposed. It will not be necessary for the standby to become involved to the same extent as the nominated executive, but he would be simply kept informed and provided with up-to-the-minute reports on progress.

Figure 10.2   The performance barometer

An essential early warning signal for eventual sales performance can be provided by establishing the relationships between inquiries, quotations, orders and sales at the time of developing objectives. Normally, for most companies, there is a time-lag between the receipt of an inquiry and the conversion to sales. If time periods can be established by products for each of these steps from inquiry to sale, it is possible to provide early warning of sales volume according to the time-lag. If inquiries during one period achieve only 80 per cent of forecast, then, without remedial action or change in conversion, sales to 80 per cent of forecast will be achieved. Indications in advance of sales shortfall give management the opportunity to investigate quickly a cause and take any necessary action to rectify the situation and, where possible, to concentrate effort in order to either shorten the normal time-lag or to improve the conversion ratios.

Ideally, remedial action should be incorporated into the plan from the outset and implemented as soon as justified according to terms specified in the plan.

Figure 10.3   Management control ratios

This is a comprehensive illustration which includes far more standard controls than will be used by

FIGURE 10.5

SUMMARY OF RESULTS

DATE:

PREPARED BY:

OPERATING RESULTS	CURRENT PERIOD			COMULATIVE THIS YEAR			
	Budget	Actual	Variance	Previous Year	Budget	Actual	Variance
Total Sales							
Orders on Hand							
Orders for Delivery							
Orders Planned							
% Performance							
Gross Margin							
Gross Profit							
General Admin.							
Manufacturing							
Overheads							
Central Marketing							
Branch Organisation							
Total Company Profit							
Interest							
Net Profit Before Tax							
% Net Profit Before Tax							
Taxes							
Net Profit							
% Net Profit							
Provision for Dividends							
Transfer to next Period							

FIGURE 10.6

PROFIT PLAN

DATE:

PREPARED BY:

Prior Year Actual		ITEM	Current Yr Budget	%	Current Yr Latest Fore-cast	%	Plan Year One	%	Plan Year Two	%	Plan Year Five	%
		Total Assets										
		a) Debtors										
		b) Stock										
		c) Work in Progress										
		d) Plant, Machinery										
		e) Land and Buildings										
		f) Other Assets										
		Capital Investment										
		Orders on Hand										
		Net Orders Received										
		Orders Carried Forward										
		Net Sales										
		Standard Costs										
		Gross Profit										
		Marketing Expense										
		Administration & Overhead										
		Total interest & financial charges										
		Other expenses										
		Net Income before Taxes										
		Taxes										
		Net Profit										
		Home Sales										
		Overseas Sales										
		Established Products										
		Planned Products										
		Market Share										

most companies. It is, however, although extensive, only a representative indication of the many guides and monitors which can be introduced into the company. The guiding principle for any management ratio is the fullest consideration of the standards against which ratios are to be compared, and the use to which management can employ the ratios in carrying out its everyday task of management. The chart suggested is most significant to the company's accountant who will need to determine the effect of marketing action on the total company operation.

Figure 10.4   Computer printout
There is no reason why information produced by a computer should be indecipherable for management control purposes. Management information systems processed through a computer are intended to be an aid to decision-making and should provide only information presented in such a way as to fulfil its major objective. The printout illustrated in this diagram is one produced through a computer terminal used for its simplicity in operation, and flexibility in use.

Figure 10.5   Summary of results
This illustration is a much-abbreviated version of a company's profit and loss account with additional information provided and is used as a regular periodic document for senior management.

By quoting information for the current period and relating it to the information for the year's performance to date, the manager has available a vital control document from which immediate action is indicated, where necessary, in the cost centre or activity which is at fault.

Figure 10.6   Profit plan
This illustration is a reconciliation document and is a much refined final development emanating from the financial objectives presented in Figure 1.1.

The profit plan expresses a useful summary, in financial terms, of the company's future prosperity and how it is to be achieved. Before this form can be completed, it is necessary to undertake the investigations, recording, appraisals, and development of the other documents presented. Not all of the illustrations used are critical in the preparation of a company's marketing plan, but the principles inherent in their use are necessary if the full fruits of marketing planning are to be fulfilled.

Published Statistics and Information

COMPANIES
Companies' House
Dun & Bradstreet
Exchange Telegraph Co Ltd
Fortune
Investors' Chronicle
Kompass Register
Linkon Investment Services Ltd
Moodies Investments
Opportunities for Graduates
Retail Shops and Stores Guide
Stock Exchange Year Book
Times 1000
Whitaker's Almanack
Who Owns Whom

COUNTRIES
Banks
Chambers of Commerce
Export Credits Guarantee Department
Embassies and Consulates
United Nations

GENERAL
Anbar Document Service
Aslib Directory
British Institute of Management Library
Central Office of Information
Directory of Trade Associations

Economist & Intelligence Unit
International Advertising Agents
Local Export Clubs
Market Research Society
National Newspapers
Professional Institutions

MARKETS
Basic Economic Planning Data
Business Intelligence Services
Embassies and Consulates
International Publishing Corporation
Market Intelligence Library
Television Companies

ADVERTISING
Advertising Quarterly
Audit Bureau of Circulations
Audits of Great Britain
British Rate and Data
Harrison Library of the Advertising
   Association
Jictar
Legion Publishing Co Ltd
Marketforce Ltd
Media Expenditure Analysis Ltd
National Readership Surveys
National Survey of Business Equipment

Opinion Research Centre
Poster and Outdoor Services Co Ltd

INDUSTRIES
Department of Trade and Industry
Economist Intelligence Unit
Gower Economic Publications
Industry and Careers
Moodies Industries and Commodities
National Economic Development
  Corporation
Trade and Technical Press

GOVERNMENT
Accounts Relating to Trade and Navigation
  in UK
Board of Trade Journal
Business Monitors—Department of Trade
  and Industry

Censuses of Production, Distribution and
  Population
Digest of Regional Statistics
Economic Trends
Family Expenditure Survey
Monthly Digest of Statistics
National Food Survey
National Income and Expenditure
National Plan
Overseas Trade Accounts
Registrar-General's Statistical Review

PRODUCTS AND SERVICES
A C Nielsen Co Ltd
Exhibition Publications
Kelly's Directories
Kompass Register
Trade Directories
Trade Press Supplements
Yellow Pages

APPENDIX 2 CUSTOMER PROFILE

Name _____   Phone _____

Address _____   Telex _____

_____

_____

Associated Companies _____

Bankers _____

Number of Employees _____   % Annual T/O ____ %

Standard Industrial Classification _____

£ _____ Gross   £ _____ net

Sales _____ %   _____ %

Public/Subsidary/Private/Partnership/Other

Estimated Overall Market Share _____ %

Historical Growth Rate 19 – 100 _____ Sales

_____ Profits

Floor Space   Office _____   Works _____

DECISION TAKER/MAKER

Taker	Owner	Maker
	M.D. Board Committee Co. Secretary Office Manager Buyer Parent Company	

Rating of Management | A | B | C | D | E |

Known Applications _____

Likely Applications _____

Present Purchasing Power _____ £ _____ P.A.

Prospect Rating | A | B | C | D | E |

APPENDIX 3

OVERSEAS COUNTRY PROFILE

Country _____ Population _____

Capital City _____ Political Stability | A | B | XXX |

Major Products or Commodities _____

_____

Gross National Product 1960 = 100 _____ £

Per Capita Income 196 £ 1960 = 100 _____ £

Currency_____ Reserve Currency_____

Conversation Rate £ _____ $ _____ DM _____

International Trade

	Country			Country			Country		
	Imports	Exports Balance		Imports	Exports Balance		Imports	Exports Balance	
196									
196									
196									
197									
197									

Source _____

Climate Hotest _____ °C _____ Coldest_____ °C _____

Seaports _____

Airports _____

Major Competitors Native _____ Sales

Foreign Owned _____ Sales

Foreign _____ Sales

Imports of Competitive Goods £ _____ Exports of Competitive Goods £ _____

Taxes/Duties/ Tariffs

Prospect Rating | A | B | C | D | E |

Index